Hacking the Corporate Jungle

How to Make More, Work Less, and Actually Like Your Life

Sean McMann

Copyright 2024 by Sean McMann.

Published 2024.

Printed in the United States of America.

All rights reserved.

No portion of this book may be reproduced, stored in a retrieval system, or transmitted in any form or by any means – electronic, mechanical, photocopy, recording, scanning, or other – except for brief quotations in critical reviews or articles, without the prior written permission of the author.

ISBN 978-1-957077-79-6

Publisher's Cataloging-in-Publication data

Names: McMann, Sean, author.
Title: Hacking the corporate jungle : how to work less , make more and actually like your life / Sean McMann.
Description: Includes bibliographical references. | Parker, CO: Book Crafters, 2024.
Identifiers: ISBN: 978-1-957077-79-6
Subjects: LCSH Work-life balance. | Job stress. | Self-management (Psychology) | Work--Psychological aspects. | Self-actualization (Psychology) | Conduct of life. | Corporate culture. | Organizational behavior. | Success in business. | BISAC BUSINESS & ECONOMICS / Workplace Culture | BUSINESS & ECONOMICS / Personal Success | SELF-HELP / Personal Growth / Success
Classification: LCC BF481 .M36 2024 | DDC 650.1--dc23

Publishing assistance by BookCrafters, Parker, Colorado.
www.bookcrafters.net

To my sons, Langston and Laurence.
May the risks taken here forever inspire you to never stop dreaming.

The stories described in this book are from the author's own personal experience. Any inaccuracy in description or failure to capture the full complexity of any one person is solely the fault of the author himself. Names and some minor details have been changed to protect the privacy of those depicted.

Table of Contents

PREFACE..1
INTRODUCTION..7

PART 1: Hacking How You Think About Work

CHAPTER 1 | THE PROBLEM..11
    End of Chapter Exercise:...17
CHAPTER 2 | OUR CORPORATE JUNGLE...........................18
    End of Chapter Exercise:...24
CHAPTER 3 | THE WORK BELIEF.......................................25
    End of Chapter Exercise:...31

PART 2: Hacking to Work Less

CHAPTER 4 | HACKING YOUR EMAIL................................35
    End of Chapter Exercise:...42
CHAPTER 5 | MEETINGS, MEETINGS, MEETINGS............44
    End of Chapter Exercise:...49
CHAPTER 6 | REAL WORK ONLY.......................................50
    End of Chapter Exercise:...55
CHAPTER 7 | THE REAL SECRET OF OUR SUCCESS..........56
    End of Chapter Exercise:...59

PART 3: Hacking to Make More

CHAPTER 8 | FASTEST PATH TO MORE $$$......................63
    End of Chapter Exercise:...67

CHAPTER 9 | MANAGING THE BOSS LIKE A BOSS..................69
   End of Chapter Exercise:..76
CHAPTER 10 | MOVING NEARBY..77
   End of Chapter Exercise:..83
CHAPTER 11 | LETTING GO...84
   End of Chapter Exercise:..89
CHAPTER 12 | FORTUNE FAVORS THE BRAVE....................90
   End of Chapter Exercise:..95
CHAPTER 13 | COMPLAINERS NOT NEEDED.......................96
   End of Chapter Exercise:..99

PART 4: Hacking to Actually Like Your Life
CHAPTER 14 | GOING FOR GOLD..103
   End of Chapter Exercise:..107
CHAPTER 15 | THIRTY MINUTES FOR FULFILLMENT.......108
   End of Chapter Exercise:..118
CHAPTER 16 | LANDING ANOTHER MENTOR....................119
   End of Chapter Exercise:..128
CONCLUSION..130
ACKNOWLEDGEMENTS...133
APPENDIX A: LEARNINGS WHILE WORKING....................135

Preface

"Change is the essence of life; be willing to surrender what you are for what you could become." - Reinhold Niebuhr

IT WASN'T LONG BEFORE MY REPUTATION STARTED TO PRECEDE ME. In the grand scheme of my career, I was only two and a half years in, and contrary to many of my colleagues, I always got a raise. Some years, I got two. Officially, the company only gave out annual raises. Still, unofficially, they consistently awarded me and those like me. Frequently, colleagues would whine about their 2 or 3 percent raises. A few even complained about not getting one at all. Meanwhile, I was sitting at 8 percent, 12 percent, or in the year I got my largest promotion, a whopping 32 percent. In short, I was clearly crushing it. But how?

Having a rebel without a cause attitude my entire life, I often wondered how someone who didn't always do what he was told, often turning in 'required training' and other 'busywork' late, could keep getting rewarded. At first, I began to see my upward trajectory as a fluke, the luck of the draw, or the fact I was benefiting from some form of favoritism. After all, for some unknown reason, I could be my boss's favorite, and we all take better care of people we like. However, as time went on, I began switching teams. My immediate supervisor changed with each move, and I still kept getting raises. That's when I realized I must be doing something different than others.

At one point, I even launched my own company. Between work and launching my own side hustle, I had to hire an assistant to keep up. Raising funds through a Kickstarter campaign and managing a manufacturer in China who was producing my first 300 units, I often didn't start my day job until 10:30 or 11 a.m. Surprisingly, even during this time, I STILL got a raise. Meanwhile, my colleagues continued to complain, this time about how much was on their plate. How they were too busy to even visit the grocery store, let alone start a side hustle, attend their daughter's recital, or visit their parents. I was flabbergasted. How could I spend one to two hours a day working on a side business, learning code, or reading a book on business strategy and still be one of the top performers?

Admittedly, it wasn't without moments of heat. I remember the first and only time my boss approached me fuming. He had just gotten off the phone with a notorious client of ours. She was brilliant but didn't like it when the person in charge of taking care of her (me) didn't pick up the phone. To make matters worse, she also happened to be our first client. She was the one who had given my boss a chance. She had paid for him to launch his product, inadvertently funding the entire team that now boasted an 85 percent profit margin. A margin that became the basis of his own successful career. In other words, If I missed any client's call, it should not have been hers.

Needless to say, to avoid this sort of thing throughout the rest of my career, I learned to always pick up her call, and through that realization, my first corporate hack was born. As I learned time and time again through the years, doing work and doing the right work to get you what you want or where you want to go, are too often very different things. This book will help you see the difference between the two so you can reorganize your day, spending more time on the work that matters.

My Credentials:

Ever since I can remember, I have lived by a general set of policies:

#1: Rules are meant to be broken.

#2: If you are going to listen to someone, you should have enough information to accurately judge if that person is worth listening to, but always assume you are missing something, so leave room for magic. After all, everyone has secrets.

#3: The passage of time has always proven almost everything we know to be wrong. So, instead of assuming things are right, assume they are wrong and focus on making them better. After all, what else is there to do?

Preface

To that end, throughout this book, I will be as brutally honest as possible. I will start by breaking all the rules and give you a breakdown of the numbers (money) because, let's be honest, that's why you picked up this book anyway. From there, I'll move into personal stories from my own life and career—stories that help illuminate how I came to be a director so young and why I quit suddenly to write this book. These stories also help explain how I came to develop the rules and habits outlined herein—habits that, if practiced daily, will help you work less, get more done, and begin to enjoy and savor your time in the corporate jungle.

By sharing the ups and downs, twists and turns, and roadblocks encountered throughout my journey, I hope to help provide a map, or at the very least, a template of what things can look like. One that might give you some grace, reassurance, and patience when you think things aren't working as expected. Moving from the thrilling, almost constant excitement of campus life to the nerve-racking and often monotonous carousel of a nine-to-five job was one of the most significant life transitions I'd ever gone through. If you've been in your career for a while, you've likely already forgotten how big a transition this was. If you're still new to it, you certainly don't need me to remind you since you're actively living it every day. Either way, by sharing pieces of my journey in the most honest way possible, I hope, at least in part, to help show you you're not alone.

Upon writing this book, I make either $130K, $200K, or $0 a year. The difference in income just depends on when I wrote each specific chapter. Over the span of eight years, I increased my annual income by $154K, working at a large corporation that boasts an average annual raise of three percent. I accomplished this all while in my twenties. At any point, I either manage a team of four people, all of whom make over $115K, or only one who makes more than $120K. Or I manage no one and spend my time reading and writing books, enjoying my first of what I expect to be many breaks from work. The topic of which might deserve a book of its own. ;)

I have been part of four corporate reorganizations and have had more than nine bosses. I've experienced firsthand good and bad leaders. I can tell you some are crooks, but the overwhelming majority are genuinely good people enslaved in a crooked system.

Preface

Navigating this system myself, I've learned how to keep my integrity, speak my mind, and keep getting raises, all while figuring out how to work less and avoid time-wasting busy work. I'm happy to report that I've also transferred to other teams outside my immediate knowledge base (while still getting a raise) and even skipped a few steps on the corporate promotion ladder (even when some dumbass tried to block me—more on this later). Together, we'll help you find the fastest path to more time and more money, but be warned—we won't get there by doing what we're told. We're not going to get there by doing what everyone else is doing.

If you really want this, then you will need to prepare for uncomfortable days, weeks, or even months ahead. The reality is that there is something very wrong with our society, and it starts with how we spend the majority of our time. If you're like most people, you spend the majority of that time working. This means our first objective is going to be getting you to work less.

As we'll cover in later chapters, a lot of the work we do on a day-to-day basis is hamster wheel work. This means that the faster or more we do, the more we are given to do. In some industries, the more we sit around doing nothing since our time is already bought and paid for by our employer. That means our next objective is going to be doing less work. Particularly the work that doesn't matter. The work is a waste of your time and everyone who has to supervise you during that time.

So, if you're a time management and productivity enthusiast, you should know this book might not be for you. This book is not about how to outsource your work to some other country. It's not about how you can build the perfect morning routine, and it's certainly not about how you can do all the things. There are hundreds of books on these topics, and you should read them if your only goal is to get more pointless work done, whether that be directly or through the labor of someone else.

Instead, this book is about doing work differently so you can do less of it, accomplish more, have enough time to live life and learn how to thrive. It's about moving out of the culture of constant competition and profit to the culture of a rewarding life that allows you and everyone around you to thrive. It's about hacking corporations by changing how you manage your day, and it's about doing this in a nonstandard way.

It's about understanding the entire system so you can overcome the obstacles that are and will come up in front of you. It's about tapping into all of your knowledge, getting creative, and realizing a 40-hour work week is more than 100 years old, and there is nothing about it that makes you more of a moral person.

It's about prioritizing what you focus on, and above all, it is about power. It's about taking it back without permission, and it's about the idea that we don't need government, economists, your boss, or anyone else telling us what day job earns us the right to be happy, healthy, and safe. As Mahatma Gandhi said, "A non-violent revolution is not a program of seizure of power. It is a program of transformation of relationships, ending in a peaceful transfer of power."

By reading this book, I hope you'll consider joining the non-violent revolution against work. Specifically, the work we shouldn't be doing in the first place.

Introduction

"If you listen to your fears, you will die never knowing what a great person you might have been." - Robert Schuller

AFTER I HAD WRITTEN THE FIRST DRAFT OF THIS BOOK, as all authors must do, I began sharing its contents and the ideas captured within with the world. Initially, I had set out to write a book to help corporate workers get away from all the bullshit and do the work that mattered. Our retirements depended on (more on this to come) the work that they would actually feel challenged, appreciated, and thereby enjoy doing. However, as I kept talking, pitching, and rewriting a central theme kept appearing time and time again.

Whether or not the person I was talking to worked in corporate America, they all seemed to experience parts of it, and they all seemed to share a disdain for those parts. College professors talked about the 30 percent increase in administrators in the last decade; teachers talked about the additional Vice Principals. And those in charities and non-profits reminisced about how things used to be before they got all corporate. It was through these conversations and the burning of all my savings that I realized how this book needed to be different.

Yes, like other books of this genre, there is time management advice, spanning step-by-step guides on how to manage your calendar, email, and conversations with your boss. There are numbers showing how short your life is and how little time you really get in hopes of inspiring you to stop waiting for retirement and live your best life now. There are even anecdotal stories from my own successful career to help illustrate points and help comfort you, knowing I, too, understand the madness that accompanies such topics.

However, there is also something very different and unique about

Introduction

this book. Unlike those other books that seemingly speak from a place of hype, echoing the cree of hustle culture that you can *do it all yourself* if only you work a little harder, this book discusses and points out a few things that we'll all need to do together. These are things that sound big and scary, impossible, or even unprecedented, but are desperately needed all the same. After all, fixing a culture, one as viral, toxic, and, dare I say, as fatal as the corporate one we feel seeping into all aspects of our society, can logically only be fixed by the masses of that culture itself. In other words, this book proposes fixes that will require a lot more from you and everyone you know than just waking up early. It's going to require a level of societal cooperation and coordination never seen before—arguably unprecedented and truly evident of a spiritual and intellectual awakening.

In addition to this book giving you ways to work less, make more, and actually like your life, it's also going to give you ideas and action plans on what we need to do as a group, as a people, and as a workforce encompassing both boss and employee, in order to truly fix the corporate culture none of us like. Somewhere, I heard that America's greatest economic export is its culture. If that is the case, I fear we are giving the world a virus, one that I deathly hope is not too late to cure. This virus uses the word 'corporate' to disguise the fact that, at its core, it's a recycled version of fascism. So please help me be the cure. Contrary to popular belief, none of us can do it alone. No matter how hard we work.

Sean McMann
February 14th, 2024

Part 1:

Hacking How You Think About Work

Chapter 1 | The Problem

"Our deepest fear is not that we are inadequate. Our deepest fear is that we are powerful beyond measure. It is our light, not our darkness that most frightens us." - Marianne Williamson

I REMEMBER THINKING I HAD LOST MY MIND when the corporation I worked for explained that their single biggest goal during the COVID pandemic of 2020 was to keep as many jobs as possible. Between the global pandemic, political movements, and environmental disasters, I remember thinking people had lost their damn minds. Really, that's our biggest focus? The world seemed like a dumpster fire, and our number one focus was to keep everyone working. Even if what they were doing was pointless or utterly soul-crushing?

Just as I thought things couldn't get any more confusing, they did. Everyone around me, almost in unison, began praising the company I worked for. Keeping us employed was suddenly a sign we worked for a great company—one that cares. Quickly, my ability to work and my choice to show up every day were being used interchangeably with my employer's morality. I was the one able to roll out of bed and work, but they were good and moral because of it. Admittedly, it wasn't long before I began drinking the corporate Kool-Aid too.

Granted, I did have a lot of things to be grateful for. I could work remotely full time, keep my family quarantined almost indefinitely, and afford all the work-from-home amenities that every blog everywhere said you needed to have. Because of the pandemic, I got to see my sons take their first steps, say their first words, and grow from babies into fully talking, thinking, and yelling little toddlers. In effect, I appreciated my job because of its ability to pay my bills while allowing me enough time to catch glimpses of my kids' development happening in the next room.

The Problem

As lucky as I was, there was still this feeling in the bottom of my stomach. Almost a lump in my gut that was strongest right before and after bed. Sunday nights were the worst. At first, booze helped to dull these feelings. Then, I attributed them to circumstance. It was all too easy to attribute this inner pandemonium overshadowing every aspect of my life to the pandemic and the crazy conditions that ensued. Yet, as things began opening up, as life slowly returned to normal, the feelings didn't leave.

Desperate for an easy, convenient solution, I began looking for another job. After receiving a great offer and then an even better counteroffer, I eventually decided to stay put. But an almost inaudible voice in my head kept whispering it's not the job; it's everything else. The next idea that followed was clear: there must be something wrong with me. How could there not be? I could spend time with my family, pay my bills, and purchase anything my heart desired. I had it made. Yet, no matter how much I said this to myself, that sinking feeling, the one screaming in the pit of my stomach, didn't stop.

I can't remember what finally led me to speak it out loud. Thinking back, it remains a mystery. I imagine it was some event, dream, or other message from another place that pushed me over the edge. To my surprise, once I started talking about it, almost everyone else agreed. In fact, they felt it, too. As children, we were all told we could be whatever we wanted. However, as adults, it seemed like we had all already accepted our fate.

Being forced to trade our time now for the hope we'll have enough money later is an uphill battle—diminished each year by ongoing inflation. Yet, none of us seem to really know how to fix it. In fact, a lot of us have given up, surrendering to the illusion we can't fix it. Or worse, we try to delude ourselves into thinking there is nothing to fix. So, we medicate, distract, and ultimately succumb to the life we're told we are supposed to want.

Unfortunately, I had already seen too much and could no longer go back. If I continued to suffer this fate in silence rather than look for a solution, I would be dooming my children to do the same. In that moment, I made a decision to leap off the ledge and never look back, investing full force into solving what some considered an impossible problem. Little did I know how much my journey would entail. From researching the origins of money to exploring the founding principles of our current economic system to investigating the subconscious motivation of my own psyche, my journey led to a startling discovery. The game is rigged, and we're all in on it!

As any child quickly learns at recess, the best way to not lose a rigged game is to refuse to play. But how do you refuse to play a game that forces you to pay bills? Furthermore, how do you refuse to play a game that you've been taught throughout your life and you have no choice but to play? The game not only proves your worth but is the same one that everyone else plays all the time. To choose not to play is choosing to be alone for eight hours a day, homeless and destitute, or worse.

In 1930, an economist named John Maynard Keynes predicted that by 2030, due to labor-saving technologies, the average worker would only need to work about fifteen hours a week. This means that his grandchildren's biggest obstacle (that's us) would be finding things to fill their now ever-larger leisure time. Maybe this explains why, throughout history, the only cause all political leaders have seemed to agree on is employment. Not knowing how they themselves would handle so much free time or what we'd demand from them, politicians instead focus on ensuring we all have jobs—explaining why we hear about jobs every election season. This guy added 500, or that one passed legislation that eliminated 1,000. In fact, no public official has ever launched a platform on fewer jobs in the history of humanity, at least not that I can find.

Admittedly, at face value, this makes perfect sense. I mean, who would vote for that person? I wouldn't; I have bills, family, and people who rely on me. I live in the real world, and we all know we need jobs to pay our bills. Still, this doesn't explain why one politician hasn't run on a platform of more leisure time. Or earlier retirement, or a better, more reliant social security program. To that end, it also doesn't explain why my mind seemingly rejects those ideas too. Shouldn't I want all of them? Shouldn't we all?

It's like the world, myself included, has a fetish for hard work and a natural distrust of others having to take care of us. According to the *Oxford Dictionary*, a fetish is a form of sexual desire in which gratification is strongly linked to a particular object or activity.[1] Like all fetishes,

---

1 *Oxford English Dictionary*. (n.d.). *Fetish* definition & meaning. https://www.oed.com/dictionary/fetish_n?tl=true

the more I looked into this one, the more bizarre details I found. Most notably, if you don't want to participate, you're more or less forced to by having to find some way to pay your bills.

If you can't imagine paying your bills with any less than you already make, you resign yourself to a life of looking forward to the weekends, hoping you'll be able to afford your dreams *someday*. Sadly, I meet far too many people like this. Eventually, the conversation turns to what they do, and then they inevitably admit that it's not what they'd like to be doing, but it pays the bills. At first blush, they seem like the lucky ones. This is an easy conclusion to make when compared to the single mother struggling to put food on her table.

Stranger still is when we begin comparing these people to the ones who like their jobs. The preschool teacher, art instructor, white water rafting guide, park ranger, or barista who has told me they flat out love what they do. These people often don't understand how the majority of us can do jobs we dislike. The rest of us struggle to comprehend how they survive off such menial wages. It's like we've all accepted the assumption that each one of us needs a job. Those jobs come in only two flavors: you get to make a lot of money, or you get to make a difference and like what you do.

In the book *Bullshit Jobs* by David Graeber, David proposes the theory that in today's modern world, two out of every five people are stuck in work that is purposeless and, as a result, suffer psychological damage from the torture of having to show up continually and do such work.[2] Before writing and publishing the book, he first took the initiative to post an essay on the subject online. Guess what? It quickly went viral! As he worked on the book, he discovered how valuable it is to view the use of one's own time—not only for themselves but for society as a whole.

As much as we'd like to pretend sometimes we don't need each other, we do! So, when one person is suffering psychological damage because of their work, it affects them and the larger mental health of society. Put plainly, we're all so obsessed with making sure we can pay our bills that we're not discussing how our jobs are actually hurting our own health and the health of those around us. In fact, if you are one of the very brave souls who have the guts to quit a high-paying job that you hate, you're,

---

2 Graeber, D. (2019). *Bullshit Jobs: A theory*. London: Penguin Books.

in effect, simply letting some poor schmuck suffer this fate instead of you. Not to mention, you're also going to need to take a pay cut.

As if this isn't confusing enough, remember John Maynard Keynes, the economist who said our biggest problem would be finding things to fill our now ever-larger leisure time. He was technically right. In fact, the only critics of his theory say he couldn't have predicted the rise of mass consumerism. Let's be clear: these critics are not arguing that his theory of "labor saving technology" developing so rapidly was wrong, but that he couldn't have predicted the rise in all of our bills. After all, that's what consumerism leads to—more bills, more inflation, and more taxes.

Suffice it to say, this led me to a rather simple yet somewhat funny initial answer to our problems. We all have such a fetish for work because we actually have a shopping addiction. So, to solve our problem, we simply need to stop shopping. Being an economist led me to a brand new problem, one that was well understood by one of the greatest American tycoons in history. The same tycoon who some credit with single-handedly shepherding in the current forty-hour work week.

In 1926, Henry Ford, in support of a shorter work week, said, "It is the influence of leisure on consumption which makes the short day and the short week so necessary. The people who consume the bulk of goods are the people who make them. That is a fact we must never forget, and that is the secret of our prosperity."[3] At that time in history, child labor was a thing. The workday was fourteen hours, and the workweek was six full days. Yet, Ford had somehow figured out that his company needed customers with enough leisure time to drive their cars in order to keep growing.

With Ford's support, the eight-hour, five-day workweek was born. With it came more leisure time, a massive economic boom, and a legacy that endures to this day. Together the world learned a lesson: a healthy economy depends on people having free time, which means my rather comical yet simple answer of shop less to work less is almost a doomsday prophecy. We all understand that times get tough when the economy is bad, and there is probably no faster way to make the economy bad than if we all stopped shopping. No matter how much free time we have.

---

3 https://en.wikisource.org/wiki/Henry_Ford:_Why_I_Favor_Five_Days%27_Work_With_Six_Days%27_Pay

The Problem

As you might guess, my next theory started from there. Maybe to work less, we should just all shop more. Credit card debt be damned; we're helping the economy! Based on what we learned from the events in 1926, the reason working less is sustainable is that people buy more when they have more time to enjoy what they buy. But the modern era being what it is, shopping more just to improve the economy seems almost irresponsible. Given the increasing number of environmental disasters, melting ice caps, and the mass extinction of most species on Earth, consuming more now seemingly comes at the expense of the planet.

Ironically, this coincides with the fact it's easier to do so now more than ever before. With the invention of AI, automated machinery, two-day guaranteed shipping, autonomous grow farms, completely robot-managed fulfillment warehouses, and the soon-to-be-expected invention of self-driving trucks, it's like the economy is perfectly organized to regularly provide heroin to a nation and world full of heroin addicts. To use John Maynard Keyes' words, these labor-saving technologies are enabling and maybe even fueling our shopping addiction.

By now, you are close to seeing the total magnitude of the dilemma. The earth needs us to shop less so we stop killing it. However, our economy needs us to keep shopping to keep it healthy. We all have to choose professions that are either meaningful or pay really well, which forces us to choose between liking ourselves or being able to afford a healthy lifestyle. Our politicians have no idea what a society with free people who make daily decisions not based on fear of paying their bills even looks like, so they vote regularly to maintain the status quo.

Not to mention the fact there are some very rich, very powerful people who presumably make a lot of money from this ongoing dilemma. Arguably, money was the only reason Henry Ford even changed things in 1926. More people with the time and money to afford and enjoy their cars meant more money for Ford! It literally was a win-win for everybody! So, the question is, what is the win-win now? More importantly, how do we get there?

The short answer is we're going to need to change a lot. The bulk of which can be categorized in one of two ways. What you, as an individual, need to do, and then what we as a larger society need to do. For the first part, we are going to start small by hacking your day. In no time at all, this will improve your life. With enough of us doing it together, our economy and, ultimately, our entire society will quickly follow. At this point, the politicians will have to join the bandwagon. Then, all together, we'll be able to make the larger changes to society, which we all desperately need to stop feeling this way. C'mon, honestly—you can't think it's normal for one-third of us to be on antidepressants.

If you're not a computer geek, relax. I'm not going to ask you to write any code, and I don't expect you to know how a decentralized network works. You don't even have to know how to use ChatGPT or MidJourney.

You can start today, no matter your current job or pay scale. You just have to be consistent. Do the best you can, and whatever you do, don't stop; play the long game. A few missed days is no excuse for a missed life. You've survived a global pandemic, countless political movements, various scandals, and an ongoing environmental catastrophe. You can do this. One day, one decision at a time.

End of Chapter Exercise:

1. We accomplish so much, without ever giving ourselves proper credit. So for our first exercise, I want you to take 3 minutes and make a list of everything you accomplished. Start with what you did this morning, then yesterday and eventually expand to everything you did this year, the past 5, etcetera. Go back as far as you can. At the very least, you should have 'graduated from grade school' somewhere on your list.
2. Write down everything you accomplished, even if it's non-work related. If you had kids, write it down! Got married? Write it down. Lived and moved in 13 apartments, write it down! Got divorced, write it down. We are all moving so fast, that we often forget to slow down long enough and properly observe how much we've done and how far we've come. Whether the accomplishments are good, bad, or somewhere in between, you keep waking up and moving and you deserve credit for that.

Chapter 2 | Our Corporate Jungle

"A comfort zone is a beautiful place - but nothing ever grows there."
- Anonymous

It was a cold February day in Denver when I suddenly realized that giving the next thirty to fifty years of my life was the life plan that was set up for me. It was my first day in corporate America. I spent the morning in HR training and meetings, being taught all about the great company for which I was now working. My new colleagues and I had all just arrived back from lunch, and we were learning how to set up our retirement accounts. The thirty to fifty-year plan was guised in something called a "target date retirement fund" where you essentially pick the year you want to retire.

Having to pick between a handful of options ranging from 2044-2064, I looked around the room in shock and disbelief. Surprisingly, no one else seemed to notice what we were discussing. Not a single soul in the room seemed to be freaking out like I was. No one else seemed to think, having graduated college not months before, that this was alarming. I felt like I had been duped. Up to this point, my whole life was geared toward graduating college. Now that I had, they were already selling me on my next "life plan."

Over the coming years, I'd start to see this plan much more clearly. In addition to trading the youngest, healthiest, most vibrant years of my life, there were disclaimers everywhere about *earnings not being guaranteed*. In other words, retiring after dedicating the next thirty to fifty years of my life was the best-case scenario!!! If some greedy asshole decides to take over in the meantime and buy himself a new yacht instead of offering me and my colleagues a stock option plan, there was absolutely nothing stopping him from doing that.

Most of us know something is very wrong with corporate America and how it works. Yet, like our day-to-day feelings toward work, we've all seemingly accepted it's just the way it is, which isn't at all that surprising. In fact, corporations spend a lot of money embedding themselves into our lives to the point we hardly notice them. At times, it's all too easy to think they are an unstoppable force. From product placement in the cartoons you watched as kids to major celebrity endorsements, corporations are literally everywhere now.

Henry O'Loughlin, founder of BuildRemote, has researched how much major corporations actually own. According to his findings, twenty companies own basically everything you can buy.[4] From the programs on your TV to most of the products available at your local grocery store, their influence over our lives goes far beyond just money and economics. With the current state of democratic elections in the US, most of these companies are able to donate to our politicians. Meaning they have influence over politics, education, healthcare, child-rearing, and even the availability of birth control.

Add a few of the major tech firms, including the ones that control what information you can find on the internet (Google & Microsoft), what products can be shipped to your door (Amazon) to how you socialize and share updates about your life with friends and family (Apple, Facebook & Instagram), and it's easy to see how corporations influence and even directly control entire aspects of your life.

Maybe you don't work for a major corporation and purposely shop locally whenever you can, avoiding all the big box stores and retail websites. If so, it's likely you are in the top percentile of income earners since, typically, this means you're going to be spending more on the same stuff. Regardless, it might be tempting to think corporations are something so foreign and separate that you don't have to worry about them. They are someone else's problem, not yours. After all, you put in a lot of work to live a life separate from them. Unfortunately, this couldn't be farther from the truth.

Even if you don't work in one, the culture that they permeate often sets the standard and precedence for all others. For example, if you work in a small company, there is likely a big corporation in your market that

---

4 O'Loughlin, H. (2023).17 *Companies That Own Everything (Well, Just About)* - Buildremote, buildremote.co, https://buildremote.co/companies/own-verything/.

either competes directly with you (for both employees and customers), supplies to you, or hires you in some limited capacity. If you live under a rock and forage all your own food, then it is possible that corporations will not affect your day-to-day life. But since globalization has brought the best (and worst) of corporations to practically every corner of the globe, the chances of this in our modern age are nearly impossible.

Knowing they are and influence things everywhere, it should come as no surprise that their ubiquitous nature has seeped so far that now most of our own retirements depend on them. Thirty to fifty years of active labor is what I was picking that day in February, but under the surface, I was actually pledging my life in support of the corporate structure. The reason was that my retirement plan, the very vehicle that would enable me to remain comfortable when I could no longer actively work, was also all made up of corporations. As of March 31st, 2023, these plans collectively held $35.4 trillion dollars.[5] That is, a whole lot of people are pledging their support and betting on corporations to supplement their retirement instead of social security. This is an extremely scary prospect since, contrary to popular opinion, corporations don't have a great track record of success.

Seventy years ago, their average life span was sixty-one years. Now, it's just eighteen (and shrinking).[6] This isn't to say the executives who run these firms aren't doing their best. Not only do a lot of them work far more than the average worker, but they also spend tons of money every year recruiting the best and brightest to support them in their objectives. However, a flawed game is flawed, regardless of how smart or how hard any of the players work.

In today's world, it's no wonder the majority of us pick a thirty to fifty-year retirement plan instead of freaking out. It's so easy to see these problems as unsurmountable. It's also really easy to buy into the dogma that things could be a lot worse, so we pick the date and move on. Then we leave the room and spend those years working, earning, and paying our bills. If someone raises their head and points out how flawed and nonsensical the game is, we constantly remind them and thereby

---

5 Investment Company Institute - https://www.ici.org/statistical-report/ret_23_q1
6 https://www.imd.org/research-knowledge/disruption/articles/why-you-will-probably-live-longer-than-most-big-companies/#:~:text=A%20recent%20study%20by%20McKinsey,S%26P%20500%20will%20have%20disappeared.

ourselves that things could be a lot worse. We then mutter excuses like *I have to have a job. How else am I going to pay my bills?* to justify our decision time and time again.

In our defense, these excuses are all too easy. To the point, it's practically not a choice at all. Walking away is nearly impossible since all of our money is tied up in this system. Worst yet, most of us start in the negative. Under the current economic game, most of us have some form of debt before we even finish schooling. Whether that be student, credit card, or auto, we start our adult lives technically and financially behind.

If you live in the United States, odds are any money you do have is tied up in some type of retirement, investment, or real estate endeavor. It could be in a 401K, IRA, annuity, some kind of government pension plan, or some sort of property ownership (like your home). All of them mean your money is essentially locked away until you've sold your home or until you've graduated from your thirty to fifty-year sentence.

If you are part of the lucky few who are financially free, you still get dragged kicking and screaming back into the system—since every year—you can always rely on getting a tax bill.

In fact, regardless of the amount (slightly positive or negative) of money you do have, you and everyone you know can always rely on seeing that tax bill. Leading us to another nonsensical truth about the current economic game. The truth is that corporations and the super-wealthy don't pay many or any taxes at all. This fact has become such common knowledge that we've all added it to the list of things that don't make sense but exist anyway.

Maybe this is why the government continually raises our taxes every year. Not being able to collect it from major corporations and wealthy individuals, they continually extract it from what we once called the middle class. Add the fact that the government expects 30-50 percent of some retirement plans to be in eventual tax revenue, and it's easy to see how our ruling government is motivated to ensure corporations perform well financially.

This could explain a number of things peculiar to our current economy, like corporations being defined as people, the ever-rising cost of insurance, AND the ever-increasing pressure of inflation. The idea is that insurance companies should make a profit, food can contain nonorganic matter, medical debt is the number one cause of bankruptcy in the country, AND the single largest asset of the wealthiest people in the world.[7]

The historical function of government is to serve the interests of the rich instead of the poor. The current economic system's bias is to maintain current wealth instead of fostering the constant creation of new wealth. The average person's general struggle to pay bills AND the silent belief that if we weren't all kept so busy working, our society would divulge into downright anarchy or violent chaos.

I hope we can all agree that avoiding chaos is a good goal for any society to have, but at what cost are we avoiding chaos? In the age of our corporate society, aimed at the sole goal of making more money, what are we left with?

We're left with a society where the current corporate playbook has embedded itself in every aspect of our lives. A Corporate society where we worship profit and, in exchange, get debt instead of wealth, sick care instead of healthcare, and a thirty to fifty-year *best-case scenario plan*. We get an entire generation of people who hate their lives, even though they are technically living the American Dream. We get a generation of coaches and entrepreneurs who are simply trying to make the most money instead of solving the hardest problems. We get a global game where we are all charging each other for everything—constantly spawning more bills, national debt, inflation, and everything that keeps us, our families, and our neighbors enslaved in the first place.

This corporate society is willing to sacrifice everything (including us, our environment, and the incorruptibility of our government) in order to achieve its goal and increase numbers on a Wall Street scoreboard. It doesn't take a PhD in economics to see that this corporate playbook stopped making sense a long time ago and maybe never did in the first place. We are so disillusioned with making more and more we seem to have forgotten what the point of it was to begin with.

It's like somehow the game I used to love, the one that caused me to go to business school, the one initially made to uplift all of us out

---

[7] Bedayn, J. (2023). States confront medical debt that's bankrupting millions. AP News. https://apnews.com/article/medical-debt-legislation-2a4f2fab7e2c58a68ac4541b8309c7aa#:~:text=For%20patients%2C%20medical%20debt%20has,the%20Consumer%20Financial%20Protection%20Bureau.

of poverty and to save us from the constant danger of the jungle, has become its own worst enemy. The jungle of our ancestors has been replaced with a modern corporate one, where a banker figured out how to own everything.

Here, dying of starvation and freezing to death is unlikely, but only if you keep paying the banker. Even still, this new jungle is not really any safer. Tigers have been replaced by heart disease. Poisonous insects and plants have been replaced with stress, insomnia, and cancer. Heat stroke has been switched out for over-exhaustion. While new threats appear constantly, the 24/7 news goes on boasting about our GDP, technological advancements, and those numbers on the Wall Street scorecard. When viewership starts to decline, a conflict breaks out somewhere far away, demanding our attention and concern—almost as regular as clockwork.

Granted, it's not all bad. As a corporate society, we have done some incredible things. We have gotten rid of dirty water and thereby radically reduced, if not eliminated, deaths due to dehydration and dysentery. We've eliminated freezing to death in all but the most extreme cases and, according to modern science, seriously extended the amount of time any of us get to live. Our infant death rate has plummeted, and we have actually cured and eradicated some diseases that used to plague our ancestral societies. Yet, just because things could be worse doesn't mean they can't be better. Furthermore, it doesn't mean we couldn't have done all of this without corporations in the first place.

Given the ubiquitous nature of corporations nowadays, combined with bills, taxes, and our obsession with more and more, we've all created a monthly subscription society that literally charges us for being alive. Hacking this subscription society is going to require a change in both how we, as individuals, and how we collectively as a society view this situation. Put simply, it's going to require us to decide if our society should even have a subscription in the first place.

Hackers know that changes if applied to the right place in a system, can have enormous effects. Becoming a hacker of our current system is going to be uncomfortable. Some people might even imply that not wanting to spend thirty to fifty years doing dumb work, attending pointless meetings, and reading emails without an opinion makes you lazy, entitled, or even immoral. It's a neat trick, one that's been used throughout history, dating back prior to the invention of economics as a separate academic discipline in 1776.[8] If you can't win based on economic theories alone, convince the workers they are immoral, inhuman, or evil if they refuse to work themselves to the bone.

Blurring the lines between an economic duty and one's morality is the same trap I fell into during COVID-19. It's the same trap we see corporations fall into over and over again. When the goal is profit and money above all else, we shouldn't be surprised when everything else gets deprioritized or forgotten. Betting one's life on the thirty to fifty-year plan is about much more than picking what date you want to retire. It's betting your life on the goal of profit above all else. It's choosing corporations over people and yearly earnings over the long-term sustainability of our species.

The definition of a hacker is "a person skilled in information technology who uses their technical knowledge to achieve a goal or overcome an obstacle, by nonstandard means."[9] If the computer lingo distracted you, don't worry. All you need to know is that you are going to be using your **knowledge** to overcome an **obstacle** within the corporate jungle all around us. You're going to do this by being creative and by being different.

By hacking this jungle, not only are you going to be improving your own life, but you'll also be contributing to the larger health of society. A society that will be much better and safer than the corporate one today. The one none of us like but have no idea how to change.

End of Chapter Exercise:

1. Make two more lists.
2. In the first list, write down everything you are grateful for in your current company and role.
3. For the second one, record everything you wish you had. Maybe its more time with friends or family, more opportunity, a better title, etcetera. The point of this exercise is to help you see clearly where you are now, and where you are going.

---

8 Smith, A. (1991). *Wealth of Nations*. Prometheus Books.
9 Wikimedia Foundation. (2024). Hacker. Wikipedia. https://en.wikipedia.org/wiki/Hacker

Chapter 3 | The Work Belief

"I believe that this instinct to perpetuate useless work is, at bottom, simply fear of the mob. The mob (the thought runs) are such low animals that they would be dangerous if they had leisure; it is safer to keep them too busy to think." - George Orwell

I MET JEREMY EARLIER THAT DAY. He was sitting at the bar, and as luck would have it, the only open stool left in the joint was right next to him. In the four hours, we talked about his companies, his family, and his marriage. Jeremy was now on his fifth beer. I was strikingly sober for other reasons not pertinent to this book. We were now discussing why he hadn't bought the small plane he had been considering for months.

Me, "Why don't you just retire? You clearly have enough to live comfortably for the rest of your life. Why don't you sell your companies, buy your plane, and live the life you've always dreamed of?"

Jeremy, "Oh, I can't. You know—the kids are about to leave for college, and my wife just bought a new car. I couldn't do that, plus what would I do all day? Besides, I'm not old enough to retire."

As I've found with friends, family, and in conversation with strangers like Jeremy, the goal of working less is not as simple as implementing a series of time management hacks. Relatively speaking, those are easy and potentially explain the vast array of books and podcasts on the subject. As I've discovered, working on this subject for years, it's much more complex than that. If I were to draw a line in the sand and identify the hard part, it's learning to be comfortable with working less. It's working less and not thinking you're a bum. It's leaving the office or job site early and not thinking you're stealing or doing something immoral. It's believing deep down in your gut that one thing done well is often better than three done poorly.

Working less is as easy as consistently cutting out early on a Friday afternoon. However, if you're not careful, you might find yourself

The Work Belief

quickly retreating back to the comforts of a fully packed calendar—or worse, slouching, practically concaving in on yourself every time you tell people what you do. Your body somehow becomes the unintentional proof of how you actually feel about your position or effort in it, which shouldn't come as a surprise. You've spent a lifetime showing up, working, and achieving in some capacity. From your very first days in school, you have been programmed to work more than eight-hour days, five days a week. After all, homework was given because you couldn't accomplish everything in an eight-hour day.

In school, you had a curriculum. You knew it would take you roughly a year to get through that curriculum, at which point, you'd get a new one. This cycle repeats year after year for the first eighteen to twenty-two years of your life. In this curriculum, you learned to work hard. If you are reading this book, it's very likely you learned, like me, that average wasn't good enough, and so we learned not only to work hard but also how to work harder than most. If you're a man, you likely also learned how to ignore your feelings along the way. Work came first, feelings came last, or not at all.

When this hard work resulted in good grades, you were rewarded with feelings of pride and accomplishment and the occasional 'good job' from teachers and parents alike. As our school journey continued, a separation began to take place. It was subtle at first, but by the time you get to college, the only people around you are the ones who also get good grades. Hard work and achievement not only became part of your identity but were now woven into the very foundation of your social group. In essence, you belong to the group that works hard and achieves.

By now, this cycle of work and achievement had built a very strong feedback loop inside your brain. One that provided a delicious dopamine hit each time you went through it. This could explain why working less and thereby adjusting that dopamine feedback loop causes such an emotional and mental toll.

At first, you may be successful in dismissing such feelings. Friends, family, and loved ones might try to help by encouraging you to take a step back and rest. You've earned it. They may even remind you of your prior sacrifices or the countless infractions your employer has inflicted upon you. In my experience, both personally and with friends, family, and clients alike, this justification has a surprisingly short life span.

Typically, it's not long before those feelings of anxiety and fear become all too overwhelming. At this point, it's all too easy to throw oneself back into work, regardless of its usefulness or productivity. Anxiety, guilt, and fear start to make regular appearances. It's not long before your self-worth plummets. With these powerful feelings building, it becomes all too easy to find something, anything, just to keep busy.

Instead of doing work that matters, it becomes about doing anything just to keep our minds off the feelings. Busy quickly gets used as a measure of worth or even importance. A packed calendar suddenly provides the closest thing to the dopamine feedback loop we grew to know all too well in school.

Through all my years of working on this, I discovered that contrary to popular belief, the underlying reason why it's so difficult for anyone to work less is not because of a bad boss, company culture, or how many bills we all have. It's because all of us were essentially taught a very basic idea in school.

This idea, albeit subconsciously, gives us a clear definition of two archetypes. The first is that of the good student. The one who works hard, achieves, and earns good grades. They follow orders, listen to authority, and generally go along with what the teacher is saying.

That good student grows into a good adult, parent, citizen, and law-abiding taxpayer. As life goes on, the amount of people relying on them to continue performing this program only increases. In effect, you and other good students stay hooked on the system because of those who depend on you. If you choose to go against this at any point, you fear the consequences, ones we all saw enacted on the other archetype in school—the bad student, the one who gets bad grades, misbehaves in class, and is frequently excused for causing a disruption.

Although it's never spoken aloud, everyone understands these two types of students are destined to end up in two very different places. The bad student will end up in jail or on the corner begging for money; the good student will get to live a pleasant, free life. With these archetypes, a powerful story is reinforced. Either sign up for the thirty to fifty-year plan or end up a social outcast with limited opportunities, no healthcare, barely enough food, and potentially no freedoms.

The Work Belief

If the fear, guilt, and anxiety don't get to you, the bills will because, like it or not, a daunting fact of our corporate society is that the majority of us are in debt. Worse, the costs of that debt keep rising, as does the general costs of living.

As I took a year off to write this book, I was surprised to learn that these two factors affect everyone, regardless of their financial or societal position.

As I was reminded talking to Jeremy, the lessons we learned in school do not discriminate based on one's net worth. The people the majority of us view as *in charge*, the ones that don't have to worry about paying their bills, still use bills as an excuse. But, like Jeremy, those bills were often for other people. In fact, it seemed like the more successful the person, the more people they had depending on them to keep working, and thereby, the more trapped they felt.

As Jeremy experienced, parents had to keep working to care for their family. Tenured bosses had to keep working because their employees counted on them for their very livelihoods. Fathers and mothers alike had to ensure their kids were taken care of. Those recently promoted had to keep working since they were finally getting what they deserved. For them, working less now was even more inconceivable as it could somehow jeopardize everything they had already sacrificed.

Regardless of circumstance, work was like an over-the-counter drug everyone was hooked on. Whether or not any particular person still needed it or what their initial underlying symptoms were, they kept taking it anyway, justifying their decision later. Bills, loved ones, and time already invested were just the most common spoken aloud and accepted reasons.

As if all this weren't enough, even religions get involved. In Christianity and Catholicism particularly, a solid work ethic is equated to virtue in verse, "Idle hands are the devil's workshop; idle lips are his mouthpiece."[10] Setting aside the fact this verse doesn't say anything about work being the only suitable way to keep hands busy, the general underlying lesson is clear. Keep working and stay busy, or run the risk of defaulting to evil.

Albeit subtle, the implication that people are bound to do the devil's

---

10 Bible Gateway. (n.d.). Bible gateway passage: Proverbs 16:27-29 - living bible. https://www.biblegateway.com/passage/?search=Proverbs+16%3A27-29&version=TLB

The Work Belief

work when they have too much free time is alarming. Yet, it's seemingly accepted by everyone. In fact, there are few things that make you more deplorable in our current economic jungle than being lazy or bad at your job. With school and religion enforcing the same underlying message, it's no wonder leaders seem to believe it as well.

In the last few decades alone, multiple US presidents have been heard on record saying something to the effect of "if we eliminate all those jobs, what would all those people do?" This is another classic echo of our childhood upbringing and surrounding belief structure. People (students) need to be told what to do by leaders (teachers). Apparently, people figuring out what to do all day for themselves is not a viable option. Politicians, not knowing what an alternative society would or could look like, are also being taught all of these beliefs, like the rest of us, to do their jobs and keep it running. Plus, they often have bills, too.

With leaders, both executive and political alike, more or less enslaved to the same ideas, they continue. Advertising, pharmaceutical, and technology companies eventually focus on reducing friction, discomfort, and the painful side effects produced by such a system. Over time, these companies evolve to keep their adult users numb, distracted, and so dependent that the thought of anyone leaving becomes unimaginable.

Instead, we ignore our feelings or pop a pill and then pick staying busy over anything else. Just like in school, staying busy and being good means at least forty-plus hours of work a week. If work requires more, it's not a problem. After all, you've done homework all your life. What is a little email at night?

When you're not working, you're flooded with messages from the advertising agencies. With advertising more ubiquitous than corporations nowadays, you practically have to be superhuman to ignore them. In this industry's infancy, it learned and perfected its tactics like all do. Discovering celebrities and people with enviable lives was useful in selling more products; it used examples like Warren Buffet and Kylie Jenner to feed itself. No, you don't really need 120 billion ounces of shampoo or 30 different shades of makeup, but Warren, the billionaire and Oracle of Omaha investor, advises every journalist and news outlet everywhere that people should live below

The Work Belief

their means and save all they can. And dammit, Costco gives you the most bang for your buck.

So now, you have a closet full of shampoo and makeup in hopes the pennies you saved will make you a millionaire. A bathroom cabinet full of medications in case the feelings become too much to shove down. A packed calendar full of meetings and other activities to keep yourself busy. A closet, garage, or home full of stuff you don't need and hardly ever use. A school record affirming you're a diligent worker and, thereby, a good person. And a persistent underlying feeling that something is wrong, but you just don't know what.

Like Jeremy, your life is likely some combination of what you think you need to do, what you want to do, and the bills you have because of both. Put another way, your life is a compromise between what school, religion, and the prominent figures of our society have convinced you to do and what you and your own feelings and intuition know you should do. Like Jeremy, more often than not, we listen more to the outside world than we do to ourselves.

Like other time management and self-help books, I am going to teach you another way to manage your day and organize your life. However, unlike other books of this genre, I'm not going to teach you this so you can work more. I'm also not going to teach you this so you can work less but at someone else's expense. Instead, I'm going to teach you this so we can rewrite our societies' curriculum together. If the crumbled remains of our ancestral homes have taught me anything, it's that we need to try something different. Given the popularity of computers and the recent advancements in AI technology, I think it's only fitting to have the path connecting where we are today to the new and different place we are going to be led by hackers. Hackers like you and like me.

As I discovered throughout our conversation, Jeremy was the epitome of success, yet, to my surprise, he even struggled with his feelings toward work.

Work is only going to be a part of our new society, and unlike today, I seriously doubt it's going to be the biggest one. This means the first step you're going to need to take on this path to a new and different society is figuring out how to work less while still getting your job done. If you're like most, the majority of your workday is eight to ten hours filled with time wasters like:

- Email
- Meetings
- Busy work
- Activities related to pretending to work

Any remaining time is used to actually complete any of the real work you have. This means that in order to work less, we're going to need to start by decreasing the amount of time spent in these top four time wasters.

End of Chapter Exercise:

1. Start where you are. Get out a piece of scratch paper and pull out your calendar.
2. Next, look at your typical day and record how much time you generally spend on each category (email, meetings, busy work, activities related to pretending to work). If you're not sure, keep the list handy as you go about your day. Then, put it aside in a safe place. You are going to repeat this exercise after you are done with the rest of the book to track your progress and continually hone your ability and focus.

Part 2: Hacking to Work Less

Chapter 4 | Hacking Your Email

*"I'm not in this world to live up to your expectations,
and you're not in this world to live up to mine."* - Bruce Lee

JOHN SMITH, "COPY ME ON EVERYTHING. I'm not trying to micromanage or give you more work; I just need to know everything that is going on with the account."

Having met John not twenty minutes before, I'm sure I don't have to tell you that I wasn't ecstatic to receive such a request. A few weeks earlier, we had been notified that our organization was going through a reorganization, which is a fancy, politically approved way of saying a change in the order of command. Sometimes, reorganizations are large, and sometimes, they are isolated to single teams or divisions. Regardless, I knew nothing about John Smith yet, except that his request was immediately going to cost me a lot of time.

As everyone who has ever received such a request knows, the only simple part about it is how long it takes to say. If you are the one issuing it, you should know the message you're sending your colleagues is that the only opinion you trust is your own. At the time, it's safe to say I wasn't fond of John's request, but respectfully, I understood he had a job to do. He was recently hired as our newest Senior Vice President to not only pilot our reorganization but also work on pushing our newest line of products into our existing accounts. In other words, he wanted to see everything I was doing with the client so he could find an in.

The problem wasn't with John's goal. It wasn't even in my organization's underlying strategy. After all, we all know things change, and any organization that doesn't is doomed to fail. The problem lay within how he attempted to execute his goal. For one, it immediately put me on the hook to explain everything he didn't understand. For another, it put him on the hook to read every email he saw. Given this particular account was valued at $5.5 million dollars annually, reading every email was nearly impossible even for me. If one person could do it, we wouldn't have had a team of thirty-five people supporting us.

This doesn't even include all the other forms of communication. Since email is only one of many channels used today (texting, instant messages, phone calls, and social media posts, etc.), it's not only putting a lot of emphasis on one single channel; it's arguably putting it on the worst one. Invented as a side project by Ray Tomilson back in 1971, email has since become one of the most effective methods of communication, in addition to the largest potential waste of your time. According to Forbes, 65 percent of all emails get ignored, and only 14 percent are deemed important.[11]

According to Statista, over 2.9 billion emails get sent every second.[12] This translates, on average, to us checking our email 20 times a day, equating to roughly 5.34 hours daily. Like John, a lot of us think reading emails can help us accomplish our goals. So, we check email all the time, reading and scanning all that we can, frequently losing sight of what's important. As a result, we often work longer hours at the direct cost of our sanity, productivity, and overall life fulfillment.

I wish someone had explicitly shared these stats with me when I was younger. I used to spend hours organizing, planning, and responding to emails. Oddly enough, I believed that if I didn't respond promptly or intelligently enough to certain people, they would inevitably assume I wasn't smart enough or working as much as I should be. Unfortunately, very early on in my career, I had no idea who these *certain people* were. As a result, I practically lived in email, constantly being bombarded, sidetracked, and distracted by ongoing conversations that ultimately had no urgency or value to the underlying business or my career. In other words, I constantly reacted instead of being proactive and strategically building.

Like John, I had no idea what my focus should be, so I kept it on the one thing that was right in front of me, my inbox. I've found that

---

[11] Shep Hyken (2020). Sixty-Five Percent of Emails Are Ignored. https://www.forbes.com/sites/shephyken/2020/10/04/sixty-five-percent-of-emails-are-ignored/.
[12] Ceci, L. (2023). *Emails sent per day 2025*. https://www.statista.com/statistics/456500/daily-number-of-e-mails-worldwide/

when it comes to work, our families, and our very lives, we often think our problem is that we have too much to do. Instead, I've learned it's more often that we're not sure exactly what we should do. So, instead of prioritizing and going all in on something that really matters to us, we delude our attention, using the fact we're busy or drowning in email as a distraction to keep our minds off the things that should have our attention.

Knowing you likely don't care about how many emails you read or respond to in a day (or maybe you're a weirdo and really do), managing them instead of letting them manage you is the first step to working less. With 5.34 hours a day being spent on email on average, cutting this time in half is the single fastest way to work less. The trick is to know how to do it without it affecting your performance, perceived or otherwise.

Contrary to what you might believe, part of your performance is based on your immediate supervisor's perception. In other words, your boss's perception of your performance and hard work is their reality. This means that working less will require two things: 1) checking email less and 2) prioritizing certain emails over others. Emails from your boss and your clients, for example, will need to come first.

As easy as this sounds, much like John's request, it's much harder to do in practice. Further, compounded by the addiction learned in school to stay busy, email becomes all too tantalizing as the defacto time waster. As any addict knows, often, the easiest way to rid oneself of a habit is to simply replace it with another. To do that, we're going to modify your environment in order to set you up for success. We're also going to establish a simple set of rules to keep you on track when all you want to do is avoid productive work.

For most people, these rules free up time on the first day they are used. They not only formed the bedrock of my career success but have been supported through countless stories heard throughout my career and ongoing travels.

Rule #1:
Control It Instead of Letting It Control You

How many times have you sat down and thought to yourself, *I'm*

Hacking Your Email

going to answer a couple of emails and then get to work, and before you know it, it's almost lunchtime? Reading emails first thing can force us to reprioritize our entire day. Do this regularly, and your entire week, year, and eventual life is completely reprioritized based on how you're reacting to your email. So, what's the solution? You're going to schedule individual time for email on your calendar.

> **Step 1:** Schedule a fifteen or twenty-minute task/meeting labeled "Check Email" for two, or at most, three times a day.
>
> **Step 2:** When the time comes, set a timer and then dive in, devoting all your attention to email.
>
> **Step 3:** When the timer goes off, close your email. This will prevent alerts and other distractions from hurting your concentration.

The things that get scheduled get done. Your schedule should have room for email. Email should not be dictating how much room you have left on your schedule. I recommend scheduling one session right before lunch and one right before the end of the day. If it's Friday and you're trying to cut out early, schedule your last email check at 1 or 2 p.m.

Using a timer, although a seemingly small shift, will have a huge impact on you. With the timer set, you can confidently devote all your attention to the task at hand. After all, most things can wait twenty minutes. This means no multitasking! Multitasking, as proven in countless studies, reduces your performance drastically. One study even found a direct correlation between the number of tasks you do at once and the quality of their completion.[13] So put your phone in your bag, under your bed, or in another room, and don't look at it until that timer goes off.

A client who knows you only check emails twice daily is surprisingly more respectful of your time. After all, if you only check emails two times a day, you must be busy and in high demand. It seems counterintuitive, but our species is wired for this. Being less available via email will convey that you're more in demand, subconsciously implying to your

---

13 Gorlick, A. (2008). Media Multitaskers Pay Mental Price, Stanford Study Shows. https://news.stanford.edu/stories/2009/08/multitask-research-study-082409.

clients that they should be more careful with your time. It's a beautiful thing when you see for yourself how spending less time in email can make your clients better clients!

To supercharge this, close your email once that timer goes off. Don't let yourself be distracted by constant notifications. For those who work in front of a computer all day, I know this can be all too appealing. At one point, I had an entire screen dedicated to only email. This killed both my productivity and my quality of work. So, do yourself a favor and turn off your notifications or use your do not disturb settings.

On average, once distracted, it takes us five minutes to return to the flow state and completely focus again. The flow state, popularized by psychologists Mihaly Csikszentmihalyi and Jeanne Nakamura, is a feeling where you become fully immersed in whatever you are doing.[14] As Csikszentmihalyi said in their viral 2004 Ted Talk, "There's this focus that, once it becomes intense, leads to a sense of ecstasy, a sense of clarity: you know exactly what you want to do from one moment to the other; you get immediate feedback." Csikszentmihalyi and Nakamura reached this conclusion by interviewing a range of high-performing folks, from surgeons to mountain climbers to world-renowned chess champions. Whatever profession you are in, if you want to work less while still producing your highest quality of work, leveraging the flow state is the way to do it. Limiting how much you check your email is the quickest way to get consistently in the flow state.

That said, occasionally, something occurs that immediately mandates you to take action. We've all been there. You have an important client, boss, or colleague who sends you email after email. Sometimes, it seems like they are sending you emails at the rate at which their brain is coming up with the ideas. Especially with an important project or deadline on the line, it's all too easy to get sucked into responding to all of them. Or, maybe you find yourself being so overwhelmed by the rate of all their communication that you freeze and find yourself just staring at the screen for ten minutes, unable to do anything.

In these scenarios, I abide by a special circumstances rule called the *Rule of 3*. The rule is simple: when you get three emails within an hour from someone, instead of responding to them, call them. Having a five-

---

14 Mihaly Csikszentmihalyi. (2004). Flow, the Secret to Happiness. https://www.ted.com/talks/mihaly_csikszentmihalyi_flow_the_secret_to_happiness.

minute conversation is far better and more productive than spending forty-five minutes shooting emails back and forth. If you prefer typing instead of talking, bummer. Get comfortable talking to people. Wasting your time and thinking about your awkwardness on the phone is a valid reason for it is not what all-stars do. If you want to work less and still earn that raise, be a grown-up and pick up the phone. Your time is valuable, and if you don't behave like this is true, no one else will either.

You get what you are willing to tolerate. If you accept a boss, client, or colleague who wastes your time, you will get stuck with them. Don't let their poor time management control yours. If your boss or client really needs you now, they should call anyway.

As illustrated with the *Rule of 3*, email should not be used for all types of communication. So, in addition to spending less time in email, you need to improve and clarify how and why you use each communication channel.

Rule #2:
Different Communication Channels Should Be Used Differently

The easiest way I've found to remember which channel is best for what is by organizing them based on the expected time response. The following are the general guidelines I eventually adopted and found the most useful after trying many different ones throughout my career. Try them all, and see what works for you:

- Calls - For the most urgent matters. Use when an answer is needed ASAP to progress your work or keep moving forward or when you need to apologize (we all make mistakes).
- Instant Messages/Text - Second only to calls, these should be used when you need an answer on the same day but don't necessarily need it immediately.
- Email: Typical response is one to three days. When the answer is not urgent, you will get to the response when you have time. If three days go by and you still don't have an answer but need one, don't regress and think email is ineffective. As you manage your time better, your colleagues will learn how to manage theirs. If it's now urgent, use the other two forms of

communication. If not, and you have another week or two, email a reminder. Don't be offended or take it personally if you need to send two or three emails. We are all busy. Sometimes, people need multiple reminders before they eventually do something.

Rule #3:
Not Everyone is Equal

During the height of my consulting career, a few colleagues of mine used to take days off just to catch up on email. Some would even check email all through the weekend to ensure they didn't fall behind come Monday morning. Remember, you don't get paid to answer emails, and you don't get paid to read them on a Sunday night during family time. You get paid to add value. To put it another way, you get paid to take action on emails from certain people only. Not everyone is equal.

The most effective way I've learned to manage this is by setting up alerts. These alerts ensure you can stay out of email while still knowing you're going to get the important stuff. I recommend you start with only your boss and your most important and profitable client. You can always add other people as you go along. Do your best to keep this list short. In reality, there are only one or two people you likely need to respond to immediately or even within a couple of hours, and as we learned in Rule #2, you should be actively training these people to call anyway.

Combined with Rule #1, this naturally sets up a powerful combination. For example, say it's 11 a.m., and you have your first "check email" scheduled for the next ten to fifteen minutes starting on your calendar. You open up your Outlook, and since your boss emailed you last night, the first thing you see is the alert box popup with the subject line of the email from your boss. Now, instead of reading and potentially answering countless emails before getting to your bosses, you start with what's important and let everything else fall into the background.

These rules combine in many more ways to ensure your performance and effectiveness remain high while you cut out pointless and time-consuming work. Try all of them or implement one at a time. Either way, if you stick with them, I guarantee you'll reduce the time spent on email and be far more effective at your job. Plus, by practicing such a disciplined habit toward your email, you can set better expectations with clients, friends, and family.

As an added catchall, I always tell people that if I haven't responded in three days, I've missed it. Reach out again, or text me or call me this time. Remember, you get paid to add value and be effective. I have never seen a job description call out, 'required to respond to over 200 emails per day.' The reason being? Besides the fact that no one would apply for that job? It's because you don't get paid to answer emails; you get paid to be effective and to add value.

Sometimes, like with John, even folks with impressive titles get bogged down, hyper-focused, and trapped in email. By implementing the rules outlined above, you'll be managing their perception of your great work while setting up your day to clear out the pointless work, making more room for the work and outside life stuff that matters.

Don't let one person, no matter their title, stunt your career trajectory. In my entire professional career, I have never seen a contract call out "respond to all emails." Don't let anyone ruin your ability to be effective. Control your email. Otherwise, it will control you. As Steve Jobs once said, "It doesn't make sense to hire smart people and tell them what to do; we hire smart people so they can tell us what to do."

To that point, had John Smith implemented these rules, he could have saved himself and me loads of time. Instead of spending hours emailing questions every time he saw something he didn't understand, he could have deployed the *Rule of 3*, waiting for three separate topics or questions to accumulate and then calling me to discuss all of them at once—using the third rule of "not everyone was equal"—and that he only wanted to see emails from certain individuals. Either way, deploying all or any of the rules listed above would have saved us both a massive amount of time over the next few years.

End of Chapter Exercise:

1. Deploy Rule #1 of Email, *Control It Instead of Letting It Control You*, and schedule time to check email tomorrow. Follow the steps outlined above to immediately save yourself hours of pointless work. Then, close your email app and get back to work.
2. The next time you get three emails or instant messages (IMs) from someone in rapid succession or within an hour, call them instead of responding. Remember, a five-minute phone call is always better than hours spent emailing back and forth.
3. Instead of always drafting an email or IM, consider how quickly you need a response. Would making a phone call save you and the recipient time? Pick the right communication channel for the right purpose. If you're a manager, consider sharing Rule #2, *Different Communication Channels Should Be Used Differently*, with your team to increase productivity and help everyone understand that your focus is on value and productivity; it's not on the number of emails or IMs they send.
4. Create one or two email alerts for your boss and or top clients. Then trust that you'll get those first when you check your email next. If someone really needs you right now, they are either going to call or learn that they should.

Chapter 5 | Meetings, Meetings, Meetings

"Don't let what you cannot do interfere with what you can do."
- John Wooden

REGARDLESS OF WHERE YOU ARE IN YOUR LIFE AND CAREER, whether it's just starting your first job after college, being in the workforce for thirty-plus years, or anywhere in between, at some point, you will find yourself losing focus. You will get distracted with the day-to-day demands of life, family, friends, and career. You'll forget who you dreamed of becoming, and you'll lose sight of where you want to go and why. You'll compromise, and if you're not careful, that compromise, plus the thousands of others you'll make, will affect how you view yourself and your own ability.

If email is the single biggest way to waste time on the job, then attending back-to-back, pointless meetings is the fastest way to compromise your productivity and lose focus. The trouble is that it's not only easier to attend a meeting than get work done, but most of us are constantly bombarded with meeting invites all day long. In fact, if your job is not building or fixing (like as a developer, data scientist, etc.), then unlike email, attending meetings in some form is very likely part of your core job. They could be team meetings, client calls, or even appointments. In an ideal world, you would ultimately control every part of your day. Modern life and business are what they are, and we all know this is unrealistic. So, managing how many meetings we attend in a day is going to be a little more complicated than what we deployed for managing our email.

Just like with email, we commonly think the problem is that we have too much to do, and that's why we have so many meetings. However, most of the time, we have so many meetings because we don't know which ones to prioritize. In effect, we try to attend all of them instead of taking a step back and evaluating which ones actually matter to us and our jobs. Said differently, we attend all of them, so we don't have to choose which ones not to. Filling our calendars with back-to-back meetings is a surefire way to avoid the discomfort and anxiety that comes with the Fear of Missing Out (FOMO). Unfortunately, it's also a surefire way to get nothing done.

I can't tell you how many people I know and have spoken with who attend meetings all morning, every day, five days a week. They then gasp for air and explain how they finally get a moment to themselves around 2 or 3 p.m. This is incredibly unfortunate for two primary reasons. The first, contrary to popular belief, is that your attention is finite. You do not have an unlimited amount of quality attention to give. Usually, you have only two or three hours of it a day, and that's on a good day when you're presumably not hungover. The second reason attending all meetings is unfortunate is because studies show that as the day progresses, your decision-making power declines.[15] In other words, the more time and attention you spend on things that don't matter, the less you have for those that do.

In bodybuilding, there is a concept called 'cycling.' The idea is pretty simple, and if boiled down to one sentence, it's this: You can maximize your growth, avoid injury, and ultimately get better results if you give your body enough time to rest. Most people think bodybuilding is about pumping as much iron as possible. However, as any professional bodybuilder will tell you, it's not that simple. Getting the proper amount of rest is just as, if not more important, than how much iron you pump.

Your time at work functions much in the same way: attend too many meetings early on, and you'll find yourself burning out, paying less attention, and providing little to no value in most of the meetings you attend as the day continues. To solve this, it's critical that you are not only strategic about when you schedule meetings throughout the day but also about how you set them up and which ones you choose to attend.

Depending on your job, meetings will have a different level of importance for you. There is no one-size-fits-all. Even throughout my

---

15 Johnson, J. (2020). *Decision Fatigue: Effects, Causes, Signs, and How to Combat It.* https://www.medicalnewstoday.com/articles/decision-fatigue.

career, I have found that I regularly make exceptions or try out different routines just to see if something else works better for me. Furthermore, depending on the schedules of your colleagues, boss, and clients, having an earlier meeting might be unavoidable. Having said that, I have found the following rules to supercharge my results while still enabling me to work less.

Rule #1:
No Meetings Before 10 a.m.

Mornings are hectic for a lot of people. For those with kids especially, getting everyone to school on time while ensuring lunches are packed and everyone has what they need is a monumental task in and of itself. Throwing a phone call on top of it is the definition of cruel and unusual punishment. Think about it. Do you really think they are paying attention if their kids are in the car? That's not to say that an early phone call once a week will kill you, but doing it regularly is not only a waste of time but a surefire way to drive people away. Think of it this way: would you rather have people on the phone at 8 a.m. appearing to work or calm, focused, and ready for a productive session by 10 a.m.?

Don't let the amount of time people are on the clock fool you. Being busy and attending a lot of meetings does not equate to productivity or value added. Like in bodybuilding, if you push too hard, you're going to end up with injuries instead of gains.

Rule #2:
No Blank Meetings

Nothing is more of a colossal waste of time than attending a meeting with no purpose, summary, agenda, or even one-sentence blurb of information regarding what it's about and what it should accomplish. You wouldn't go into the jungle without a plan, some tools, a map, and even a guide. Most of us don't even travel around our own neighborhoods without using Google maps first. The reason is that we're headed out to run errands and accomplish something; we're not out to waste time.

This same logic needs to apply to your calendar and the meetings that fill it up. Generally speaking, all meetings you schedule and attend should have a minimum of three things:

- Title
- Purpose
- Ideal Outcome or Next Steps

For example, say you are scheduling a meeting to talk to your boss about a concern you have. The meeting could look like this:

- Title: Sean and Emily: Concerns Discussion
- Purpose: Discuss my concerns on the new project deadline for client X.
- Ideal Next Steps: Outline clear and concise next steps to get the project back on track or agree on the proper way to notify the client of the new project deadline.

This sets clear expectations upfront with your boss regarding what you'll need from the meeting in order for it to be a productive use of your time. It also clearly shows the urgency, knowing that if your boss doesn't want the project delayed, they shouldn't reschedule the meeting.

Typically, we have meetings in order to learn things from people who know more than we do. So, if you don't know all of these items upfront, don't schedule the meeting. Instead, either seek out more people and information before scheduling it or list your questions in the purpose section of the meeting. Often, people think they need to have all the answers before setting up a meeting. Sometimes, scheduling a meeting is the fastest way to get answers. Just don't be surprised if people talk more than usual. I've found that questions often spur conversation, and starting with answers often shuts it down completely.

Since meetings are inherently social, after all, you don't attend meetings with just yourself; you'll also need to know how to handle it when someone else schedules meetings.

Rule #3:
Don't Attend If Anyone (and I Mean Anyone) Breaks Rules 1 and 2.

Generally speaking, regardless of the person's title, if they haven't given you and everyone else in the meeting enough information to know what it's about before you attend, you shouldn't. Now, I know when I say this, younger employees often get uneasy. They fall into the trap of not saying no to someone who outranks them or even owns the company. That's fair; if declining a meeting without enough information makes you generally uneasy, then simply reach out to the person who sent you the meeting invite and inquire what it's about.

This will not only separate you from a lot of your colleagues and improve your reputation, but it will also give you a direct line of communication with someone higher up. This is key if you want to make more money, as we'll cover more in the second section of this book. The truth of the matter is, if you don't know the expectations for the meeting, odds are the other attendees don't either, which means nothing is going to get decided, and you can afford to miss it. Think of it this way: reading a three to four-minute email brief is a better use of your time than chit-chatting for thirty to forty-five minutes and then departing with no clear outcomes and shared learnings. A poorly planned meeting is very likely going to be a poorly executed one.

When deciding whether or not to attend an early morning meeting, do so consciously. Will you be in the middle of breakfast, not alert, or, like me, dropping the kids off at school? Catching the train or running to catch the bus? As we covered in the last chapter, multitasking decreases the quality of work on every task you try to do simultaneously. So, ask yourself, can I attend this meeting and give it my best attention and work? If not, decline it or ask to reschedule it until later.

Combining these three rules will immediately shave hours off your week. In some cases, they may even shave hours off a single day. While you're simultaneously getting rid of poorly planned meetings, you're going to be reducing the amount of multitasking you do, thereby increasing the quality of your work across the board. You're also going to be freeing up your cognitive energy for the things that matter most, both in your career and in your life.

End of Chapter Exercise:

1. Look at your calendar over the next week. Ask yourself honestly if you spend more time in meetings than actually working or thinking. Do you always have early morning meetings, causing you to wake up and immediately feel stressed? Do you give yourself breaks between meetings? Even five or ten minutes can have a huge impact, even if it's just going to the bathroom, getting in a quick walk, breathing, or thinking about what value you'll be bringing to your next one.
2. Having taken stock of your calendar, are there meetings you can cancel? Can a quick phone call serve in its place? Are there recurring meetings that always run long? In instances where someone else owns these, share the meeting template from above. Position it in a helpful way, saying something like, "I noticed we always run long on these meetings. I think we can try using this template to keep us on task while allowing us all to get what we need faster." In my experience, this will not only set you apart from your colleagues but help everyone you interact with be more focused and productive.
3. Last but not least, are there blank meetings you can decline? In my experience, if the meeting organizer really needs you in attendance, they will often follow up with you directly, giving you a chance to ask questions regarding the purpose and envision the next steps of the meeting. This will also give you a chance to subtly set expectations that unless you know what a meeting is for, you won't be attending.
4. For the meetings you own specifically, go back and add a purpose and envision the next steps. Lead by example. If you don't know them, add your open questions or cancel the meeting and get answers first. Be respectful of other people's time, and they will become more respectful of yours.

Chapter 6 | Real Work Only

"It is quality, not quantity, that matters." - Seneca the Younger

IF YOU'VE REACHED THIS POINT IN THE BOOK and have implemented at least one piece of advice shared herein, you have undoubtedly already freed up a significant portion of your time. No longer obsessed with how many emails you answer or write, you're now only checking your inbox twice or thrice daily. You're no longer attending meetings without a clear plan, and you're ensuring the ones you set are easier for everyone to understand and contribute to in a meaningful way. You know that multitasking reduces your performance, so you focus on only one thing at a time whenever possible. Regardless of how many meeting invites you've received or unread emails in your inbox, you know that doing too much of either will quickly kill your productivity.

Having significantly reduced or entirely gotten rid of a lot of the time-wasting crap that keeps you trapped, you now have more time, energy, and attention to give the stuff that really matters. The trick is deciding what that is. The first step is often realizing that the things that truly matter are far fewer than the options usually presented. The most cited and popular theory on this idea is probably from Italy.

The year was 1897, and Wilfredo Pareto, an economist, published an idea based on his observations. It had to do with land ownership in his home country. Noticing that 80 percent of it was owned by 20 percent of the population got him wondering if such a distribution applied to other things. Today, that law has been applied to a wide range of disciplines, including economics, computers, business strategy, crop production, and a whole host of other industries and domains. In fact, it's so integral in how people think of business today that one can't earn an MBA without learning about it.

Pareto's Law, more commonly known as the 80/20 Rule, is likely something you have already heard of. Unfortunately, knowing about it is simply not enough. Actions speak louder than words, and when it comes to work, we all know there are often too many possible actions to choose from. The question becomes, what 20 percent should you focus on to produce your 80 percent reward? A problem so widespread and common that it afflicts entire companies no matter their size or age.

To analyze the stark contrast between how actions get prioritized and done in highly successful startups, Jessica Livingston interviewed over thirty-two of the most successful startup founders in modern history. Interviewing such huge names as Max Levin of PayPal, Craig Newark of Craigslist, and Steve Wozniak of Apple, Jessica's book *Founders at Work* is a must-read for any aspiring corporate hacker. The book is essentially a list of interview questions and answers up close and personal with some of the most successful people in business. Most insightful are her findings regarding productivity. Calling out that "in its plain form, productivity looks so weird [in the early days of these highly successful startups] that it seems to a lot of people to be 'unbusinesslike.'"

Paul Graham mentions a general principle in the forward of the book that he believes applies to people when working. Paul says, "The less energy people expend on performance, the more they expend on appearances to compensate." In other words, if you don't work a whole ton, then you probably spend a lot of time appearing like you do. In later sections of this book, we'll get into things you can do to fill up your newly found free time to avoid this pitfall. But for now, we're going to focus on how to best pick what you should be doing in the first place.

As illustrated by Pareto and echoed in books like Jessica's and countless others throughout the last decade, the trick is about picking the one or two things that matter, going all in, and letting all else go. Remember, this isn't another typical time-management self-help book. It's not about getting all the things done faster and then cramming in more after the fact. It's about slowing down, focusing, and doing the one or two most important things to the best of your ability.

By now, you know this means fewer emails and fewer poorly planned meetings where people appear busy but, in fact, get nothing meaningful done. Depending on your circumstances, what might surprise you is that this will also very likely require you to deliver things late and potentially not at all. It's going to require you to prioritize those one or two things above all else.

For those of you who have been paying attention up to this point, you might have noticed that multiple times throughout this book, I have instructed you to keep your mornings open. For example, in Chapter 4, I recommend not checking your email until after 11 a.m., and in Chapter 5, I recommend that you avoid scheduling and attending meetings before 10 a.m. whenever possible. The reason is that those one or two hours before your first meeting or first read email should be spent on the one or two things that matter most.

The key to working less is really not all that mysterious. It's a simple matter of doing what matters most first and then walking off the job or leaving your office once you've completed any other things you need to do that day. It's about working instead of pretending to. After all, how we spend our days is how we spend our lives. So, start prioritizing your life. When you first get into work, do the one thing that matters before anyone else invades your brain with other ideas or priorities.

Obviously, if you're doing this every day, over time, you'll get better at it, and eventually, doing the things that matter will be easier and more natural. Having said that, if you're struggling to get started, you can follow the process outlined below.

How to Pick Your 20%

Step 1: Either take a look at your job description (if you still have it) or make a list of the things you were planning to do that day. Some people like to do this the day before so they know exactly what to start on when they start working the next day, but I've found myself equally as productive when I simply think about the one thing I need to get done on my way to work.

Step 2: Depending on what you're looking at, there are likely anywhere between five and fifty things on that list. Now, ask yourself, *if I only had time for one thing, what would it* *be?* If my house caught on fire, or my kids called me in an emergency and I immediately needed to dash out of the office or leave, what would be the one thing I'd need to be done today so I wouldn't have to start in the same place I am now tomorrow.

Step 3: Do it. Don't get distracted. Don't fall into the trap that doing five other things is actually more productive because they are quicker or easier to do. Instead, focus, take action, and do that one thing. Don't worry about what you're going to do next or the order in which you'll complete the other things that are not as important on your list.

The more time you spend planning, the higher the chance you'll fall into the trap of pretending to work instead of actually doing it. Do the one thing that's important, and then reevaluate. I've found time and time again that doing the one thing that matters often puts into perspective what needs to be done next anyway. If it doesn't, simply repeat the steps above.

I've found that the one thing is always the most time-consuming, hardest, or scariest thing to do. Making it all the more easy to avoid until later in the day or later that week. Remember, your goal is now different. You're prioritizing that one thing first because you're no longer trying to do all things. You're no longer trying to appear busy or productive. Instead, your goal is to actually be productive. No longer in school, you don't have to abide by a nine-to-five schedule. As long as you do the things that matter, you will be able to work less, get more done, and be a happier and healthier person.

If you're not a morning person, and you know that instead of getting your best work done from 8 a.m. to 10 a.m. every day, you'd simply sleep in, play video games, or fall back into the trap of email, that's okay. We're all different, and sometimes getting your best work done at 2 a.m. is just how some of us are wired. To that point, it's critical you replace my schedule with your own. The odds are that even if 8 a.m. works great for you right now, your schedule is bound to change at some point. To help with this, I recommend completing the following exercise either now or again when your schedule is forced to change for any multitude of reasons.

Finding Your Peak

Step 1: Get a piece of paper or make a new note on your computer or phone. On it, you're going to list each hour of your workday on the left-hand side. If you start at 9 a.m. but don't stop answering emails until right before bed, then your piece of paper should have every hour from 9 a.m. to your bedtime. This is important: notice I did not say to list out every hour you're *technically supposed to be working*. I said, list every hour between when you start work and when you're done with it for the day.

Step 2: Now, looking at your list, write next to the time if any hours are special. For example, if you have a lunch break, put that next to your noon or more appropriate slot. Do you have a morning coffee break or time in the afternoon when you typically run out to pick up your kids? Or maybe you read email on the train back home at night? For now, just write any non-work-related activities at the appropriate time. Based on my examples, you'd put "commute" in around the 8:30 a.m. slot, lunch by your 12 p.m. slot, pick up kids next to 3 p.m., and then make dinner at 7 p.m.

Step 3: Looking at this list, circle the hours you think you do your best work. Not when you do any work, but when you do your best work. Pretend for a moment you're a heart surgeon. Circle the hours where you'd be comfortable operating. If heart surgery grosses you out, you can think about when you would schedule an interview. What times would you be most impressive and alert—most prepared to make the best impression?

Step 4: Over the coming week, observe how you feel during each hour and evaluate if you are truly alert and most adept at the time you circled. If not, take note and circle the time you are. The goal here is to start observing yourself honestly in order to get an idea of when you feel the best and thereby do your best work.

Step 5: Once you're confident you know the general time frames in any given day that you're at your best, you're going to schedule sixty to ninety minutes during that slot to *get your one thing done*. If you only need ten minutes for the one thing, then repeat the *How to Pick Your 20%* steps over and over again until your sixty to ninety minutes run out.

The goal is to work uninterrupted and totally focused for as long as possible. As time goes on, don't be surprised if things don't nearly take as long as you originally expected. Multitasking not only reduces performance, as stated earlier, but it also results in things taking longer. So, focus completely and get more done in sixty to ninety minutes than you might have done in an entire week prior.

As we all know, habits are incredibly powerful, and habits amplified by your body's natural chemistry and circadian rhythm are a surefire way to do your best work in the most efficient way possible. From here, all you have to do is keep showing up and putting in the time. Everyday. Don't allow fake emergencies or dumb distractions on social media to steal your attention. Don't even allow the fact that Monday was a holiday to give you an excuse to skip it on Tuesday in order to catch up on email. It'll all be there waiting for you anyway when you're done doing your most important thing to the best of your ability.

After Chapter Exercise:

1. Complete the steps outlined in How to Pick Your 20%.
2. Complete the steps outlined in Finding Your Peak and spend the next week observing and fine-tuning.
3. Schedule the items produced in Step 1 during the times found in Step 2.
4. Repeat over and over again to start doing your best work in the most eficient way.

Chapter 7 | The Real Secret of Our Success

*"Fascism is not in itself a new order of society.
It is the future refusing to be born."* - Aneurin Bevan

THE TRUTH IS, THE NEW CURRICULUM LAID OUT in this part of the book is going to give you a butt load of free time, and that free time is going to first make you feel like something is wrong. In fact, you're going to feel a lot of things like fear, guilt, boredom, and shame, but don't be fooled; this isn't because something is wrong with you. It's not because our society will crumble if you continue working less, and it's certainly not because you're committing any sort of crime. It's because all of your life, you were taught you needed to work to earn. You needed to work and stay busy to be a good student and to stay safe. And it's because, through 200,000 years of existence, we have learned to fear change.

For the first time in history, people have more options, choices, and freedom over their individual lives than ever before. Supposedly gone are the days of lords, masters, and divinely appointed kings and queens with total control. Instead, and in their place, we have private interests, corporate lobbying groups, and wealthy individuals that focus on profit above all else. This, plus the fact our population is the highest it's ever been in recorded human history, leads to a peculiar puzzle now in front of us. One, we have by all accounts, never solved before. That said, we do know something.

Our planet is riddled with the remains of societies from years past. Although in some instances, we know an impressive amount based on the limited artifacts found, in the grand scheme of all the details of their day-to-day lives and the inner workings of their complex societies, we know very little, if anything at all. This means, regardless of where you stand on the rumors and speculation about how the pyramids were built,

The Real Secret of Our Success

or why, or what sort of technology Atlanteans had, you can surely agree with me on one thing. When it comes to building sustainable, lasting great civilizations—all prior efforts on this planet have eventually failed.

That coupled with our species' largest known population plus the fact we have no new lands we can send those we don't like to, means that at the same time that we have our biggest puzzle of survival, we know without a doubt that none of our prior solutions are viable options.

Although initially appearing bleak, it does mean we can surely stop listening to those who think they have figured it out. As history has taught us, no matter how hard we all work, how great our society becomes, or how smart our ancestors were, their civilizations all fell in the end.

Many people in the business world copy exactly what others do because *checking all the boxes* is an accepted (and often inaccurate) hallmark of success. In fact, this same belief is at the very core of drafted curricula in schools. It is this belief that I think is at the core of why all great past societies have fallen. Trying to emulate the greatness that is all around them, younger generations try to check all the boxes instead of clearly seeing that new ones are needed altogether. Often forgetting that those who created greatness had no boxes to check at all. If we don't do something different, our relentless pursuit of checking boxes will result in ruins, just like every other great society before us.

Moving up in corporate America so quickly at such a young age showed me I didn't care about what arbitrary title I had. I didn't care how many people thought highly of how smart I was. I didn't care how much money I had made since I spent most of it anyway. No, what I cared about was how much pride those I worked with took in their efforts and in their final products. I cared about what I got to learn, experience, and accomplish, what I got to see, and mostly, what I missed out on. I cared about my sons' first steps, about their financial security, and about their ability to grow up in a better world than I did.

On February 1, 2012, *The Guardian* published an article that may help put things in perspective.[16] The article was about a nurse who recorded the most common regrets among the dying. The top five of which were:

---

16 Steiner, S. (2016). *Top Five Regrets of the Dying*. https://www.theguardian.com/lifeandstyle/2012/feb/01/top-five-regrets-of-the-dying.

1. I wish I'd had the courage to live a life true to myself, not the life others expected of me.
2. I wish I hadn't worked so hard.
3. I wish I'd had the courage to express my feelings.
4. I wish I had stayed in touch with my friends.
5. I wish that I had let myself be happier.

All too often, I see people use a meeting-packed calendar or a full inbox to justify their positions, demonstrate how much they contribute, and illustrate how busy and important they are. But being busy does not equate to value; it certainly doesn't equate to being productive during hard times. Being busy does nothing in terms of avoiding a layoff. Instead, being busy means you have a full calendar that you likely hate, and others might hate you for. So as important as cutting back your time in email, strategically approaching your meetings, and finding your peak time in order to complete your best work is, if you don't figure out how to exist when you're working less, you and the rest of us are never going to be successful.

As much as I hate to say it, at first, working less can feel a lot like work. But the goal is not to work less, to steal from the rich. The goal is to work less, so this place, this society, this time, we leave an intact known legacy instead of ancient ruins. This time, we figure out what work needs to be done so that our society will persist until the end.

As you embark on your journey to work less, expect to occasionally miss a critical meeting, email, or client call that you should have attended. Whatever you do, don't over-correct and revert to allowing anything and everyone to steal your time and disrupt your focus. After all, like in baseball, one strike doesn't mean you're out. Communication is hard. Maybe your boss could have communicated the importance of the meeting better; they could have planned better and not scheduled it for a day you had off. Or maybe, as uncomfortable as FOMO is, getting that five-second recap from a colleague was a much better allotment of your time than spending an hour on Zoom. An overview that only took one-tenth of the time the meeting did and spared you all the pointless dribble of executives who love to hear themselves talk.

I need you to work less because, contrary to the news or the lessons taught in history class, great civilizations are not made by single leaders;

The Real Secret of Our Success

they are made by the citizenship of great people. And I truly believe we can't be great if we have to focus first on paying bills and then on the future we're leaving our children.

You need to work less because it's time our society stopped repeating the continuous cycle we see all around us, as evident by the ancient ruins scattered across this planet. Just like in 1922, working less now is a win-win for everyone. Only this time, we're not going to try to sell everyone new automobiles. This time, we're going to ensure real, nutritious food is affordable for everyone. We're going to repoint the economy to our long-term survival and advancement instead of to short-term profits. We're going to change the economic game so no one is left behind, and we're going to ensure that together, we become the first global society that doesn't result in ruins.

I need you to work less because the survival of our society depends on you being alert, focused, and driven. And there is nothing gained from spending hours reading pointless emails, attending poorly planned meetings, and moving your mouse to give the illusion and appearance of hard work. The odds are stacked against us. As Henry Ford pointed out, "Leisure is the secret to our success," and the stakes at which we need to succeed have never been higher. So, cut out those meetings, read fewer emails, and free up enough time for leisure. You deserve it, and our collective success depends on it.

After Chapter Exercise:

1. Make a list of all the things you would like to do, if you didn't have to work all the time. Maybe you would help your community, plan a neighborhood block party, or visit that family member you have been blowing off for years. Or maybe you would simply catchup on sleep, or visit some historic site across the world. Contrary to the prevailing belief in our work obsessed culture, you don't need to justify your existence to anyone. Your life is yours, so make sure your list has things you want to do for yourself, in addition to the stuff you want to do with or for those you love. No one succeeds alone, and our society is only going to get collectively better if we first agree our individual lives should be better.

Part 3: Hacking to Make More

Chapter 8 | Fastest Path to More $$$

"Use the talents you possess, for the woods would be very silent if no birds sang except the best."- Henry Van Dyke

AT THE RISK OF MAKING YOU THINK BUYING THIS BOOK WAS A MISTAKE, I have a secret to share. Depending on your current job, there is no possible way for you to make more. At this point, you're probably regretting buying my book. Or if, upon reading that sentence, you naturally object and are shouting that I'm wrong. Then let me ask: How much? How much more are you expecting to make? Maybe $5K, $10K, $15K more? In how long, ten years? Do you even know?

If it takes you that long, is it worth it? Have you taken into account inflation? The reality is, if your goal is truly to make more, it's likely you should be looking not only at how much you can make in your current position but also at how much you can make in a similar but related position. For example, in data sales, I discovered that in three to four years, I'd only be able to double my salary, and that was if I hit every mark and never missed a quota. My mom and dad, of course, thought these numbers were incredible and urged me to stay put. However, after talking with a friend, I learned that by moving into data consulting, I could increase my income by over $100K in the same time frame.

Often, you can realize a $10-15K raise simply by switching companies. The trick is to know what position or company to move to. If you picked up this book to make more and work less, odds are, you need to find a new position instead of working your ass off to earn more in your current one. In most companies, this will simply result in you being given more work anyway. At this point, it becomes easy to start believing your terrible fate is a direct result of your boss.

When I was younger, it was easy to believe I was being taken advantage of. Not knowing any better, I thought the person right above me had all the power. However, as I became the boss, I realized how little power that position actually had. Contrary to how much you have earned, a company without money to spare can't give you any more. Regardless of how much you have earned in the past month, year, or decade. All work has a finite amount of money that it can pay before it becomes unprofitable.

I'm a big believer in the fact that most of us don't really know what we like until we find it. By exploring other roles and companies, you're not only going to be able to escape the trap of thinking the individual right above you is secretly evil and has all the power. With any luck, you're also going to be able to find a balance between how much money you want/need versus how much responsibility and risk you're willing to tolerate.

A new role, one that naturally garners a higher wage, is often the quickest way to earn more, and it's typically also the one most overlooked. The trick is to look for roles that require some of your existing experience and some you'd need to learn. In other words, there is no point in moving into a role for which you are totally qualified. That's a recipe for boredom, and boredom is the death of your career growth.

When people get bored at work, they do a multitude of other things, all usually unproductive to earning more and actually liking what they do. We frequently wear blinders when it comes to where we can move in our careers. I think, at least in part, the bias comes from our early years of schooling. In school, there is no way to jump from elementary to high school. You simply have to put in the time and earn it like everyone else. But in our careers, the rules are often different.

Throughout my own career, some of the best salespeople started as engineers. Some of the best engineers started as mathematicians and teachers. In other words, when thinking about how to make more or how to work less, don't just look at jobs based on what you know; explore what you believe you can quickly learn. Most managers will hire someone hungry and driven to become better instead of someone who already has ten years of proven experience. There are plenty of reasons for this, including the former typically being cheaper.

Think about it: if you have a proven track record, I have to pay you what you have already earned, plus some. But if you're new to the role I'm hiring for, I can pay you based on your old role and then some. If you made a lot less in your old role, I can pay you the least I would anyone else, and you still get a raise. That's a win-win, plus this cheapness often translates into me being more patient, considerate, and relaxed with you. After all, I'm paying you a lesser amount on the assumption it will take you some time to get really good. Once you are good, the assumption is I will pay you more. This sort of career move not only sets you up to make more upon your hiring date, but it also sets you up to keep earning raises year after year, assuming you continue growing, learning, and earning.

If the idea of changing positions or roles sounds too stressful or wrong, maybe because you love what you do, then the second best option to earning more is moving industries. For example, a friend of mine is a personal assistant. In the nonprofit sphere, she was able to earn a salary of $35K a year after three years of working in the business. In the corporate world, working for a big consulting house and serving as a receptionist to the biggest executives of the business, she STARTED at $75K.

At both companies, her responsibilities were more or less the same, but who she was working for and the underlying profit margin of the industry she was now in meant she could make a lot more. So, in addition to looking for other somewhat related roles that naturally earn more, you should also look at other industries that need your role, even if they are named slightly different.

Often, job descriptions have lines like "industry experience," but know this is the least important requirement. After all, if your boss or company has been around for years, maybe decades, they can teach you all that they know about the industry very quickly. The largest corporations have new hire training programs that do exactly this. This means they will prioritize someone who knows how to be a fantastic personal/executive assistant over someone who understands pharmaceuticals.

You might be asking, why, then, do they even ask for industry experience?

Think about yourself in a job interview. You are nervous because, in a very real sense, you are selling yourself. You are pitching all the good, amiable, and impressive traits and stories about yourself. Like your resume is your first impression, their job description is theirs. This means that even if it's subconscious, the hiring manager, HR department, or copywriter is more or less inclined to beef up the job description to attract the best talent. They also don't want to interview everyone and their moms. So, they often use 'related industry experience' to filter anybody and everybody from applying. In other words, don't let one bullet on a job description deter you.

If you want to earn more by moving into the same role in a different industry, spend a few hours over the next week researching the industry you're applying for. You'd be surprised how knowledgeable someone can come off with an hour or two of research under their belt right before an interview. The key is not to be an expert. The key is simply to sound knowledgeable enough that they decide to let you in the door.

In addition to changing roles or industries, the third easiest way to earn more is often by simply changing companies. If you have worked for your present company for a few years, it's likely you already know the names of their biggest competitors. It's also likely you know some of their smallest ones. Contrary to popular belief, you won't always make the most money by moving to a larger competitor. So, regardless of size, look at both. Sometimes, smaller companies offer more flexibility and better work-life balance. Not all business owners are trying to maximize their year-end earnings. Some are simply trying to pay their bills by working as little as possible.

A buddy of mine used to work with me in data consulting. When the pandemic hit, he quit. Overworked and too stressed to function, he took three months off before becoming a freelance consultant. During this journey, he learned (and I did through him) that there were a multitude of smaller consulting and temp agencies that needed expertise just like ours. In fact, after only four months of quitting, he closed his first contract, earning $225 an hour. That's more than three times what we were making together in corporate consulting, and he did it in only four months![17]

Before he made this move, I would have never considered working with a temp agency. After all, consultants are *too good* for temp agencies.

---

17 In corporate consulting, we made $130K a year, roughly $62.50 an hour. 225/62.50 = 3.5ish more.

Of course, they aren't, but this didn't stop me from letting my bias affect what I saw as a viable option. The lesson here is simple: don't put yourself in a box. Don't restrict yourself by thinking your skills or experience only apply to one industry, in one position, or in one size of company. When evaluating companies, don't just look at the big guys; look at them all. Even if changing companies doesn't allow you to make three-and-half times more, if you're able to make the same amount and only work half the time, you just doubled your hourly rate. So, think about what you really want. Do you really want to earn more, or do you simply want to work less? Do you want both, or maybe what you're after is something else entirely? Maybe you just want to be home for the holidays every year, and your current job makes this impossible.

Creativity is your secret weapon here. Exploring things that others have biases toward or don't even think to look at will be the quickest way for you to earn more. It's like Mark Twain said, "Anytime you find yourself on the side of the majority, it is time to pause and reflect." With so many options of where to move and what to look at, I get it; such an exercise becomes quickly overwhelming. To help with this, I've created a proven, easy-to-follow step-by-step guide to help you through this process. I've included it below. If you have any questions, please feel free to reach out.

End of Chapter Exercise:

1. Calculate your hourly rate. If you're on salary, divide it by forty-eight (weeks in the year you're working, allowing two weeks for vacation and two weeks for holidays). Then divide that by five for the number of days in a week, and then divide that by eight the number of hours you presently work in a day. Of course, if you work more, use that number instead. For example, if you make $50,000 a year, you actually make $26.04 an hour. Use this hourly rate as your benchmark.
   ### Salary/48/5/8 = Hourly Rate
2. Make a list of other companies in your same industry, marking those that pay better than yours or require fewer hours than yours.

3. Next make a list of closely related positions in your same company (positions that you can do 60-85 percent of the work already).
4. Make a list of other industries that need your current role. Next to each, add a note about the general profit margin. The higher the margin, the more likely you'll be able to make more.
5. Have fun, and apply to a few a week. If you want a longer list, mix and match any of the tactics from two through four. Doing so is a creative way to look at options others aren't.
6. Keep going. Don't let yourself give up. Too often, people quit too soon. Thinking they can easily move industries in 3 months, they suddenly abandon all hope after they have been job hunting for 4 months. Remember, the right change can completely upgrade your career and your life. So let it take as long as it takes. 2 years to make such a move, is still faster than waiting 10 years for the same pay increase in your current role.

Chapter 9 | Managing the Boss Like a Boss

"Your value doesn't decrease based on someone's inability to see your worth."
- Anonymous

KNOWING CORPORATE COMPANIES ARE OFTEN COMPRISED of thousands of people spread across multiple countries and companies, the factors that affect your job are endless. As we all know, out of all those factors, our immediate boss is the most influential on a day-to-day basis. Outside of the confines of this book, the idea of a hacker still carries a negative connotation, particularly with people who are older and higher up in the corporate system. This means that even if you love your boss, you probably can't just go up to them and say, "Hey, I want to hack how we do things so I can work less and make more. You cool with that?"

In all likelihood, they are more likely to think you're stealing from them and the company instead of understanding that you're after a new way of life. Depending on the age gap between you and your boss, the chances are even higher that they see you as naïve, entitled, or lazy. In my experience, when someone has accepted the way things are, they don't always take kindly to someone trying to make change. Either way, like a hacker, you're likely going to have to go about your plan much more covertly.

This is to be expected since most people can't envision something they have never seen before, and trying to convince them while simultaneously hacking your way to a better career and life is simply not recommended. Hacking your day is going to be plenty of work in and of itself; you don't need to add on more by keeping your boss apprised of every speed bump, roadblock, or learning along the way.

Like computer systems, corporations have some sort of hierarchy. So, to ensure you have enough time and space to hack and make more money while working less, you're going to need to ensure the hierarchy right above you is not actively working against you. If you love the company you work for and enjoy your colleagues as people, the last chapter might not have applied to you. That's okay, but before you settle in, you should first evaluate if your boss is the right one for your new endeavor.

Unfortunately, some bosses think it's their job to keep people busy. The largest issue with this is that they usually focus on managing your time instead of helping you accomplish goals. Their aim is simply to keep you busy while on the clock. After all, they are paying you for your time, and it's their job to ensure they maximize your contribution during that time. If you have tasks for your entire eight or ten-hour day, then you are producing eight hours of output. That, to them, is good math (it isn't).

In other words, these bosses are focused on output and not throughput. Think of throughput as stuff that actually helps make the company money, increase customer retention, or improve sustainability.

Frankly, it doesn't matter who you are; if the person who has direct power over you and your position wields it poorly, no amount of money or hacking is going to help. If this sounds like your boss, it's best to get a new job before you start. After all, nothing is going to cause you more headaches than a boss who starts filling any free time up with more work.

Fortunately, I've had far fewer bad bosses than I have good ones. My first was right before I graduated college, and although I liked him a lot personally, as a boss, I absolutely loathed the man. Today, managers like him are referred to as micromanagers. These types are characterized by excessive control, close supervision, and frequent criticism of employees. They often get upset when a decision is made without them and think everything needs to be approved by them.

Micromanagers

I only spent eight months under him, but it was brutal. In a word, I HATED it. Let's call him Jake. He had never done my job, but he had a very specific vision of how it should be done, even though he seemingly

Managing the Boss Like a Boss

lacked the ability to concisely explain it. The only thing that was less specific than his vision of what my job should be was the *proper* end result.

This end result, naturally, had no tie to income, money, or any sort of incoming revenue. But it was something he wanted to brag to his friends about regarding the type of company he worked for. Based on what I could tell, Jake operated on the notion that if he could get me to do Steps 1, 2, and 3, he could complete the last one and invariably take all of the credit afterward.

Throughout the corporate jungle, you can easily identify the micromanager types by their strict focus on checking things off a list. They are very concerned with everything that was done and want to see constant results for your time. They want to know that you were busy completing things for the entire time you were getting paid. If you leave early, they will often ask you to make up the time later that night or over the weekend. It's like they operate from some sort of notion that working less than forty hours is some sort of sin. If it were, then why don't they get punished each time you have to work more than forty?

I only worked for Jake for eight months, but it was easily the worst eight months of my life. Toward the end, as he talked, I often dreamed about hitting him in the face, and I'm not a violent person! My imagination would run wild, trying to envision what it would look like as his penguin-like shape buckled at the midway point, his ridiculously long nose snapping under my fist like a twig.

Somehow, I had grown to hate him, a fact that had crept up on me like a spider in the middle of the night. It was such a subtle transition. Such a gradual process; it took me hours of silent contemplation to remember how it had evolved into this in the first place. In my former position, I had been a friendly, smile-wearing barista. Jake had been one of my favorite customers. But somehow, he had turned into a pompous ass that had me dreading being alive.

Years later, and having gone to plenty of therapy, I can tell you nothing about him was inherently evil. By all accounts, he was a genuinely loving, amiable, and overall good man. To this day, I still have gratitude and appreciation for what he did for me. After all, he found, hired, and moved me from behind the counter to behind a desk. Yet, as my boss — he was the WORST.

As time went on, each day became filled with criticism, negativity, and sudden changes in strategic direction. I'd eventually realize these feelings appear when working in an overall toxic environment.

As an aspiring corporate hacker, if you're in a similar environment—get out! It's the worst environment you can be in. It's like walking through the jungle with a Bengal tiger watching you. The moment you get hurt, fall behind, or somehow get separated from the group (and you will get separated from the group), you'll get picked off and eaten for lunch. I repeat, if your boss is a micromanager—GET OUT. Move teams, get a new gig, or find a way to get fired. No job is worth your sanity and self-worth. Micromanagers are often the most opposed to their people working from home, and when they invariably lose this battle, they always seem to notice the times you aren't moving your mouse. So, my advice is to find a new boss, and quickly.

When evaluating what type of boss you have, ask yourself what their focus is. Do they focus on hitting meaningful goals, growing relationships, bottom line revenue, overall organization efficiency, and, dare I say, maybe even improving your quality of life? Or are they simply focused on how many things got done? How much do you work, and how much money can you make? There is no shame in making good money. After all, being financially secure is a big contributor to being content and happy in life, but money isn't everything, and if you work for a task focused micromanager, you're going to find hacking to be nearly impossible.

Assuming your boss is not a micromanager, the second most important thing to evaluate is how your boss sees you. Do they respect you? Do they value your insights, listen to your opinion, and speak honestly with you when they disagree? As uncomfortable as disagreement is, it's one of those secret ingredients I've found present on all high-performing teams I've worked on. People who disagree work through problems, roadblocks, and pushback before these same issues become a problem in the market or with clients. It doesn't matter how good you are at your job. If a boss doesn't respect you and share honestly when they disagree with you, you best be moving on.

Eight years into my career, I had the unfortunate luck of being assigned to such an individual.

The Disrespectful Leader

It was 6 p.m., and we were still working. Everyone had come to town to meet the new boss. A bar tab was open, drinks were flowing, and questions were getting more personal and harder to answer.

Carol, a new member of the team and one of our youngest, asked, "Why was Sean promoted so quickly?"

Having been recently reorganized under Ralph, a vice president who had been my boss for all of two weeks, I like everyone, was curious what he had to say. As we all looked in earnest, his response felt like a swift kick in the gut.

"Well, the thing about Sean is, he's a people pleaser."

For those unfamiliar with corporate speak, he was calling me a kiss-ass. If kissing ass was all I needed to become a director so young, I had clearly been playing the wrong game. As if controlled by a strong magnet in my left back pocket, all eyes in the room immediately turned toward me. As the others stared, I smiled. Ralph was a 5ft 5in Indian man with back problems, a broad smile, and a sort of mischievous demeanor.

My mind flipped through countless pages of questions, hypotheses, and potential wisecrack remarks. Should I say he was wrong? Was he? Truthfully, I had the same question Carol did. Not knowing all the justifications that supported the decision behind my quick promotions, I couldn't say if he was. With that said, I did know his response was distasteful, and I knew it was far too simplistic. Getting promoted to director at twenty-nine is not a decision any leadership team makes lightly, much less one that has a fifty-year legacy.

Having just witnessed a vice president I had never worked with try and explain a career trajectory he couldn't even boast, I was somewhat speechless. Mostly, I was shocked at his lack of tact; trying to explain my career trajectory by insulting me in such a public forum seemed far too amateur for someone of his level. As my mind kept flipping through the pages, I began to think about everything he could have said. Everything, I might have said, had the situation been reversed.

For example, he could have explained that I had closed our team's most significant contract or shared that I ran the highest profit margin accounts. He could have explained that everyone on the team looked to me for advice. Or launched into a full-blown biographical story, telling of the time I wrote a code package that not only singlehandedly got us security approval from one of the largest telecoms in the nation but, in the process, also saved a $500K contract (and I wasn't even a developer). He could have taken a different approach altogether. Instead of boasting about my career exploits, he could have focused on me as an employee and as a person.

He could have mentioned I was loyal, had the most tenure of anyone on the team, and had a fantastic reputation for being honest, open, and candid with clients. Or, he could have simply explained I had clout and approval from multiple levels and teams in the organization. In short, more than one person knew what I was worth. Of course, to explain this, he would have needed to know any of it.

As I drove home that day, I wondered more about his explanation. With a grin on my face, I wondered if he was remarking on my ability to remain polite and professional in times just as this when someone was seemingly insulting me. Admittedly, I also wondered if he was right. I didn't care for his explanation, but it did get me thinking about Carol's question. How did I get promoted so quickly? Furthermore, how did it happen without any argument?

Weeks later, I learned Ralph's boss had just spent seven years repeatedly trying to get him promoted, failing all but the last time, which led me to wonder if his answer on that fateful night over drinks contained more jealousy than fact. As curious as I was, the shift in leadership didn't just aggravate me. Over the next three months, it led to four members of my team leaving. For the time being, I had much bigger problems to worry about.

Needless to say, it didn't take long for Ralph to become impossible to ignore. From the moment he became my boss, he asked me to map out what the team did, what we could do, and if I could summarize it all in a sales deck. For anyone wondering, a sales deck with job descriptions and enough material for a sales team to go to market is what any division lead does. The only thing was that I wasn't the division lead, and he wasn't either. In fact, on paper, the division lead was his boss.

As I rallied the team, organizing countless discussions and getting all of us to agree on the work we were doing and the work we knew we could do, I delivered the final product. Next came the real question. With the roles outlined, what would I do, what would Ralph do, and what would Ralph's boss do? It didn't take much to see you didn't need all three of us, and although I was much cheaper, I was also the youngest and least experienced.

At first, I was hopeful that we'd agree on our roles amiably, but as I pressed for a clear delineation of our three separate roles, I began to glimpse what wasn't being said aloud. Finally, in a heated meeting, Ralph blurted it out. He admitted our job descriptions were the same. In effect, he and his boss would get first dibs on big clients, and I'd get anyone too small to qualify for their attention. At this point, my annoyance turned to anger. I had two options, start over and work my butt off to earn my place at the top or move on. I had poured my sweat and tears into the team, and the product that Ralph and his boss now owned, and the battle to beat them was going to take years.

No matter what stage you are in your career and your life, change is hard. As I was contemplating what to do, the timing couldn't have been worse. Three months earlier, my divorce was finalized, and in addition to needing to figure out what I was going to do about all these changes at work, I was still figuring out how to co-parent my one and three-year-old boys. Most guys I talked to blatantly admitted I was living their worst nightmare. But through all this, I learned that anything seems impossible until you do it.

Having worked for many bosses before Ralph (nine at this corporation) and six others in my prior careers, I knew what Ralph's answer meant. It meant, "You get our scraps, and if you fall in line, we'll throw you a bone." I don't mind falling in line if someone is better skilled than me. After all, situations such as these present incredible learning opportunities. Unfortunately, in the short time I worked for Ralph, it became apparent that the team he had been running for the past ten years was utterly unprofitable. Forget about his lack of tact and overall disrespect. Claiming first dibs on business while being totally unprofitable was a business sin I couldn't accept. It was like being asked to play a game of Monopoly where the banker is terrible at math. It's not fun.

Remember, bosses can do a ton of good or a ton of harm. Sometimes, these things can be right in your face, expelled in a daily dose of criticism, or spoken at happy hour in front of you and your colleagues. Other times, it can be more covert, whispered behind hidden doors, or apparent only in their managerial style. Needless to say, if your boss seems to struggle to set meaningful goals or successfully complete their own job, plan on finding another one. A boss who can't pull their own weight has no choice but to have you pull it. And a boss that doesn't respect you now is not going to respect you anymore after you hack your way to a better day.

End of Chapter Exercise:

Observe your boss over the next week or two. Pay special attention to what they ask you and what they want to know. Does your boss make your life easier or harder? Do they inspire you or make you nervous? Do they want to know what you need help with, or do they constantly need assurances that you still deserve your job? A boss who is too focused on what you're doing isn't focused enough on what they should be doing, and just because you like them as a person doesn't mean you have to like them as a boss.

Chapter 10 | Moving Nearby

"Until you have the courage to lose sight of the shore, you will not know the terror of being forever lost at sea." - Charlie Cook

WHETHER YOU WANT TO GET AWAY FROM A BOSS like Jake or Ralph, or whether you realized while reading Chapter 8 that you simply can't make more money where you're at and are looking for a more lucrative opportunity, I encourage you not to overlook the opportunities all around you. As proven throughout my career, sometimes the biggest opportunities are right next to us. One of the best things about large companies is that they are made up of much smaller ones and can provide a lot of avenues for career development and advancement. Navigating the sea of American global corporations can be overwhelming at any point, especially if you're just starting to look for a new position.

To help with this, like the other lessons in this book, we'll start small and focus on one. This corporation is called Epsilon. It's where I began my career after college. In any event, working at this corporation for eight straight years taught me a ton. A lot of which you didn't learn in school, and you'd never find in a code of conduct or on a company website. I've boiled down the most critical and insightful lessons so you can take advantage of opportunities all around you that you might not otherwise see. After all, a big part of your career success will depend on your ability to navigate within the company, industry, and network you're in. To this point, spending some time when you'd usually be working, networking can be a career game changer.

You'll have plenty of time throughout your career to leverage as many of them as often as you'd like. Just remember, Rome wasn't built in a day. Consistency is key. Show up every day, and when that voice in your head says, *wow, that's cool, I want that, or I wish I could do what they*

Moving Nearby

do, voice those wants into the universe, your network, and with your boss. You never know what opportunities might present themselves if you make your desires known.

Lesson 1: Corporations Buy Other Companies

While I was at Epsilon, our execs bought five different companies, including Conversant Interactive, Retargetly, Aspen Marketing Services Inc., Big Foot Interactive, and Yieldify. (See Figure 1).

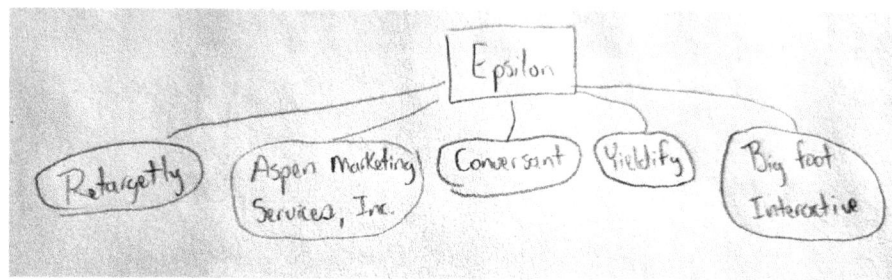

Figure 1

Alliance Data Systems owned us for the first five years of my tenure before selling us to Publicis Media. The third largest advertising agency holding company in the world, headquartered in Paris, France.

Why is this an important lesson for you?

Well, corporations buy and sell other companies for several reasons. The underlying theme is so they can make more money, and nothing adds to a stock value like a new income generator. Since bought companies bring in new people and capabilities, they also present a great opportunity for anyone looking to find a new boss or experience a new but somewhat related industry. New companies also bring in cultural change, as well as opportunities for new learning. To take advantage of these opportunities, you can deploy the following process that has served me well over the years.

How to Use an Acquisition to Grow Your Network and Knowledge:

Step 1: Seek out the new company. Start small and reach out to an employee at the new company and ask for a coffee chat. Say you're excited they are joining the corporate family and that you'd like to learn more about what they do and how they help their enterprise.

Step 2: When the meeting comes, don't reschedule. Show them just because they were the ones you bought doesn't mean you don't respect them. People are still people, regardless of whether they are on the buying side or the selling side, so treat them with respect.

Step 3: Take notes, and if they share a sales deck, a graphic, or some visual to explain what they do or how their tech works, ask for a copy. Ask if it would be alright if you share this information with your team. Don't say boss since people in unknown territory typically get skittish at the mention of any sort of authority.

Step 4: Share what you learned and gathered with your boss and your team.

Step 5: This one is key—then follow up with the person you spoke with. It doesn't have to be long or fancy. You can simply write them a quick email saying "thank you" for sharing the information, that you enjoyed the discussion and really appreciate the knowledge transfer.

Although simple, these steps are incredibly powerful. Not only does it grow your network immediately, but it will also give you talking points on what the new company does.

In other words, when Bob, at the water cooler, goes, "Hey, did you see we bought Citrix Systems?"

You can go, "Oh yeah, I did see that. I contacted a gal over there to get the lowdown on what they do. Fascinating stuff. We can learn a lot from them, or our clients would probably love to learn about them."

Plus, this strategy will have the added benefit of building you a reputation as a doer, mover, and shaker. These learnings will also help you better navigate when you do want a new job. Think about it: in a simple coffee chat, you were able to grow your network and also get insider knowledge on a particular company.

Being on the receiving end of one of these, I can tell you what you won't do. You're not going to duck every question your new colleagues ask you. You're not going to drive the conversation like a forceful dictator, and you're not going to imply, verbally or otherwise, that you or your team is more important than theirs. Instead, you will set it up to be a two-way street. Like a great first date, both teams must get close to equal airtime. If you focus on equal airtime and getting them talking, I guarantee you they are going to walk away thinking, *wow, they seem like great people. Glad to be connected with them.* Above all, treat it seriously and realize your company buying them doesn't mean you are more important. Focus on being respectful and learning all you can.

Lesson 2: Corporations Start by Serving a Flagship Market

That flagship market is often seen and referred to as the core business. Although large, your corporation has an ingrained bias as to the best way to make money. Make a note as to what this is. It will help you understand how your job fits into the overall strategy and whether you should pivot to another team to make more money, learn the business, or grow your expertise. It can also help you understand the political standing of your boss. The more important your team is to the overall strategy of the corporation, the more important your boss likely is. Having an important boss will increase your chances of getting that next raise, as bosses often have to negotiate for raises on your behalf.

To get at this information, I recommend you start by following the money. Publicly traded corporations, by law, have to share a lot of information with the public, investors, and lawmakers to ensure they are not doing anything illegal. To understand the strategy of your corporation, you can deploy all of the options below, or you can simply start with one. Either way, knowledge is power, and the more you know, the better you'll be able to make a good decision.

Option 1: Attend your quarterly earnings call. Earnings calls are typically conference calls that anyone can join, where the management of a publicly traded company reviews the financial results over the past quarter or year. Typically, executives will mention their expectations for the following year, often sharing what they are planning and hoping for. For someone like you, considering moving teams or companies within the organization, attending an earnings call can provide valuable information as to where the action is. Make sure to set your alarm clock and your coffee maker since most earnings calls are done early in the morning.

Option 2: If you don't want to wait for the next earnings call, or you're on West Coast time and don't feel like waking up at 4 a.m., you can simply Google your company's 10K. A 10K is an annual report that breaks down the financial health, assets, and liabilities of a company for the US Securities and Exchange Commission. In other words, if you want to understand your corporation's money situation at a very high level, this report is perfect for you.

Option 3: Attend your quarterly business review, annual report, or town hall. Typically, these are internal meetings only, given by the leaders of an organization for the benefit of the employees. Think of them like earnings calls, but instead of the audience being investors, regulators, and the general public, it's just for you and your colleagues. If you don't believe your company has one, ask your boss. Sometimes, companies only invite managers to these to keep them smaller. If that's the case, ask if they would be willing to forward you the meeting or talk you through a summary of what they learned afterward. In my experience, an employee wanting to understand more about the company they work for is always seen as a good thing.

Option 4: Ask. Ask your boss, your leaders, or anyone in authority. Some leaders, like Jeff Bezos of Amazon, have emails that are available to the public for questions, feedback, and concerns. It seems silly, but most employees are so afraid of their leaders that they almost avoid them or refuse to talk to them. If you really want to accelerate your career, be different and talk to your leaders. Ask them questions, and then *listen*. Learn all you can because the more you know, the better you'll be able to make a good decision.

Lesson 3: Individuals Within Any Group Don't Always Agree

Companies are not any different. To manage this, most corporations have many bets or operational tests running at any time. So, do your best to get a basic understanding of what bets your company has currently placed in order to understand what they are evaluating, testing, and keeping an eye on.

The research options explained in lesson two are a great way to do this as well. You'll find that money is a great indicator of which team is most important at any given time. Conversely, if a team is underfunded but experiencing exponential growth with a great long-term opportunity to make more money, it could be a great time to get in early and help support said growth. One word of caution: whatever you find, don't panic. Being on a high-risk team, underlined by a risky bet, doesn't mean you won't have a job next year. But it does mean your boss and company will depend on candid feedback.

As tempting as it can be at times, don't let fear of losing your job compromise your integrity. Candid, honest feedback is critical to any company being successful, and an honest employee is a valuable asset regardless of how any bet is working out.

This is why it's very important to network, meet others on teams outside your own, and start mapping out what teams are hiring or experiencing growth. Being within a corporation can often be the best place to research and understand one. After all, being behind the curtain usually allows you to see more than if you were on the other side of the veil.

All too often, I see people rush into accepting a new job and position at another corporation instead of looking around and realizing all of the opportunities their current one provides. Slowing down, doing your due diligence, and spending just an hour a week researching your company and its subsidiaries can be a huge career advantage. Accepting a new job at a new company isn't always the best way to make more money. Sometimes, it's a matter of finding the right job at your current company.

End of Chapter Exercise:

1. Spend five minutes researching your company or one of the large companies you want to work for. Draw a diagram, like Figure 1 shown earlier in this chapter. At the top, put the overall parent company. Under it, write all of the subsidiaries. Although Figure 1 only has two levels, some corporations have many more. Map out the company structure to understand how all of them are organized together. Doing so will give you an understanding of how many companies you can network with and apply for.
2. Complete the steps outlined in *How to Use an Acquisition to Grow Your Network and Knowledge*. Corporations are collections of smaller companies, so if your company hasn't made an acquisition lately, focus on the last one made or any that piques your interest. It's never too late to reach out and learn something. Most people love sharing their knowledge. If you don't work at a large company, don't worry. LinkedIn is a great tool for reaching out and connecting. Simply send them a note expressing your interest in working for the company and ask if they would have five to ten minutes to share what it's like to work there, what they enjoy, etc.
3. Spend some time looking for your company's flagship market. If you don't know what it is, attend an earnings call, find your company's 10K, or set up a call with one of your leaders. Once you have a clear understanding, ask yourself: Does your current role support it? Are you a hedge against it? This means that if the flagship market becomes smaller or less profitable, is your team one of the bets that could keep the company growing? Take note of what you find. Knowing where you sit will only help you throughout your career. Plus, knowing what bets are being made can help shed light on where the market is going and where you should, too.

Chapter 11 | Letting Go

"Too many of us are not living our dreams because we are living our fears."
- Les Brown

I WAS NINETEEN THE FIRST TIME I STEPPED INTO A LEADERSHIP POSITION. The company was called Breads of the World, the Colorado-based regional Franchise of Panera Bread. I had worked my way up to a shift supervisor and had been part of a team that had set a new record. We had opened, broken even, and made a profit, all within six months. Something that, up to that point, was unheard of in the entire history of the corporation.

At the age of twenty-nine, I accepted another opportunity to lead. Having been promoted the month before, I needed to quickly transition from being a client lead to a director and owner of a small team. I now had three direct reports, overseeing not only my clients but all of theirs. Our entire team consisted of ten people and four directors (including myself). In addition to being the youngest director on the team, I was now responsible for the most revenue. Out of all fourteen people who brought in a total of $9.5 million dollars, more than 53 percent of it suddenly rolled up under me. To say I had impostor syndrome would be an understatement.

All too often, we get accustomed to our day job. We settle in and get used to the work that's expected of us in our current role. We get comfortable, and in that comfort, we start to attach our self-worth to how well we can do our present job, no matter how temporary it might be. Whether you recently moved companies to get a promotion or you eventually got promoted at your current company, you will not be able to make more if you confuse comfort with qualification. As Will Smith said to Kevin James in the 2005 Comedy *Hitch*, "*You* is a very fluid concept right now."[18] Even when well deserved, moving into a new role, one of more responsibility, control, and money, can be one of the most nerve-racking and hardest experiences you ever go through.

More often than not, we delude ourselves into thinking that our new job comes with an impossible and unmanageable amount of work. Not knowing how to handle it, we buckle down and work harder and longer in hopes the extra effort will help us get everything done. We then spend what little time we have on the weekends complaining about our promotion. A promotion that involves more work and not enough money to justify it. Although there are undoubtedly scenarios where this is true, the bulk of them have more to do with not knowing how to approach and organize our work instead of having too much of it.

In Jeff Bezos's book *Invent and Wander*, Jeff uses the analogy of two types of doors in order to illustrate where most of us get things wrong.[19] Type 1 doors are almost impossible to reverse. They are essentially one way, and once made, there is no going back. Think quitting your job, divorcing your spouse, having kids, etc. Type 2 doors are essentially two-way and are easy to reverse. It may take some concerted and focused effort to do so, but it can be done relatively quickly and without much pain, like calling a client to build a relationship, learning a new skill, or deciding on what you want for lunch.

When most of us get promoted, we make the mistake of treating everything even remotely related to our new role like it's a Type 1 door. Regardless of how easy a decision is to reverse, we stress, justifying it as part of our new responsibility. Not wanting to be that boss who assigns everything to other people and not really knowing how to objectively look at all the items in front of us, we try to do two jobs at once.

At twenty-nine years old, now responsible for managing an intelligent group of technology experts, I learned fast that there is simply not enough time in the day to do both your old job and your new one well. I'd like to tell you I figured this out quickly and that my first year on the job was similar to the ending credits of a romantic comedy—complete with happy music playing in the background and all characters involved, leaving happier and more fulfilled.

---

18 *Hitch*. New York, NY: Columbia, 2005
19 Bezos, J. and Isaacson, W. (2021). *Invent & Wander : The Collected Writings of Jeff Bezos*. Boston, Massachusetts: Harvard Business Review Press & Public Affairs.

Letting Go

Sadly, I think the reality is that it more accurately resembled a low-budget psychedelic film, complete with experimental narratives, confusing imagery, and an unclear plot. To be blunt, the first nine months were brutal. Not wanting or knowing how to let go, I essentially worked two jobs at once not doing either very well. I was exhausted, frustrated, and too impatient with the ones in my life that mattered most.

Like a business's job is to provide value to its customers, a boss's job is to create value for their people. Like me, if you try to work two jobs at the same time after receiving a promotion, you will fail. Either at work, at home, or just in life. There is only so much time in the day. Having tried such an unsustainable model, I discovered that a boss's job comes with much more responsibility than simply trying to do all the things. As Jeff puts it, it has more to do with knowing the difference between Type 1 doors and Type 2 than it has to do with being the hardest worker or completing the highest volume of tasks.

As I waded through those nine months of hell, I fumbled my way into a step-by-step system that worked. A system that proved to grow our revenue even as our entire team shifted focus. Although I was still learning how to be a great boss, I already knew how to be a great employee. I knew what I liked about my old managers and what I didn't. Plus, I knew I liked my team way too much to let everyone down. This system led me to rehire and retrain a completely new team in less than twelve months. It worked for me in the direst of circumstances, and it will work for you, too. The key is quickly identifying what you need to do and then letting others do everything else, if at all.

System for the Newly Promoted

Step 1: When analyzing if you need to do something, first ask yourself: *If this goes poorly, could I fix it? Could I swoop in, apologize for the mistake, and then work with whomever to make it right before we lose money or go under?* If the answer is yes, it's a Type 2 decision, and as the boss, you should be assigning it to someone else.

In my experience, newly promoted people are often trying so hard to avoid making a mistake that they lose focus on what's important. Rather than relying on others, they try to do everything themselves because that's the only way they think things will be perfect. Remember, you were promoted because of how well you did your old job and how well they expect you to be able to do your new one. This means doing your old job well is no longer required for your new job.

To that point, when you're the boss, and you delegate a task or goal to someone, rip off the band-aide fast. Don't micromanage, shadow them, or tell them how to do every little step. Tell them what the end goal is, and if they need a little more guidance, share examples or explanations of how said goal is usually met. Then, step away and let them take over. You can always check in later and help put them back on track as needed.

> **Step 2:** If the work is a Type 2 decision (a two-way door) and can be done by someone else, ask yourself who could do it best. Who could just do it, and who could do it with some mentorship? Part of your job as a boss is to push people, sharpen them, and create situations where they can grow. Ask yourself, could your top performer work with someone else and thereby improve the overall skill level of your team? Or could you eliminate it entirely? Rather than delegating pointless work, could you help everyone work less by eliminating it altogether?

Remember, as the boss, your job is more complex than any one single position or person. Caring, managing, and motivating groups of people is hard, tricky, and more of an art form than a natural science. Now that you're the boss don't make the mistake of thinking your old job is more important than your new one.

> **Step 3:** If the work is a Type 1 decision, ask yourself what the stakes are. How quickly does it need to be made? Rarely do Type 1 decisions need to be made very fast. Typically, they need to be slowed down, thought about, and analyzed. If, like me, your promotion puts you in charge of a small team,

examples of Type 1 decisions could be firing someone, enrolling your team in new training, or deciding to deprecate a product line. For those newly promoted, Type 1 decisions will involve and affect the entire team and will be hard or impossible to reverse. Remind yourself regularly that these are the types of decisions you should be focusing on.

Step 4: Look at your email and your calendar. Are there things from your old job that now qualify as Type 2 decisions? As I moved up in the company, I learned firsthand that it was easier to keep doing and paying attention to my old job than it was to focus on my new one. Part of this was because I was most comfortable doing my old job. Part of it was because I wanted to believe that I was irreplaceable. My ego was clouding my judgment and keeping me attached.

Don't stunt your own career by deluding yourself into thinking you are the only person who can do your old job. Just like you learned it, someone else can, too. We're all replaceable, and as depressing as that is at times, it's also what enabled you to get promoted in the first place. So, take a chance on people, let go, and let them surprise you. Not everyone will succeed, but given enough time, someone will exceed your expectations. After all, you wouldn't be the boss right now if you hadn't exceeded someone else's. The goal of any boss should be to make themselves obsolete.

If your promotion doesn't entail a team under you, fear not. You can still deploy the steps above in order to better focus your energy and brain power toward the tasks that are most important. Too often, when we start making more money, we try to justify it by working harder and longer. Don't fall into this trap. Instead, realize you were given more money because you already deserved it. Pay increases are not granted in hopes that a worker will do something; they are granted because a worker has already done it.

End of Chapter Exercise:

Next time you're at work, before starting something new, ask yourself if it's a one-way or a two-way. Then, ask yourself if the time you need to complete it is appropriate given its type. Type 2 decisions or tasks that are easily reversible should be done quickly. We all have the same amount of time every day. The best bosses, leaders, and even employees don't treat everything with the same level of importance. Doing your best in everything is something you learned in school. Doing your best on only the things that matter is how you succeed while working less.

Chapter 12 | Fortune Favors the Brave

"Most people overestimate what they can do in one year, but underestimate what they can do in 10." - Bill Gates

MY FRESHMAN YEAR OF COLLEGE TAUGHT ME, among other things, that no business fails without warning signs. It all started with one of my roommates. He always had money and yet never seemed to work. When the rest of us were grinding, trying to survive just long enough to make it to the weekend, he always seemed refreshed, relaxed, and oddly flush with cash. Admittedly, at first, I thought he might be some kind of drug dealer. But since we lived in Denver, and he mostly avoided weed like the plague (a rather odd thing for most college kids at the time), this initial hypothesis seemed rather unlikely.

Confounded by his ability to avoid the over-exhaustion and general tiredness experienced by most broke freshmen in college, I took a keen interest in his life. As luck would have it, he worked for Ultimate Electronics. For those who don't remember, it was sort of like a bigger Best Buy or warehouse-type Mac Store. It sold every type of home electronic you could think of. Probably, the most confounding part about my roommate's life was that he seemingly didn't work there. I mean, he reported to the store for eight hours a day, some four days a week, but when speaking with him about what he did, he would answer: "Nothing."

When prompted to go on, he'd explain that the store was always empty. That it was usually just him and his coworkers goofing around all day. Over more than one game of beer pong, he admitted he was surprised the company hadn't gone under yet. That's why, six months later, when they filed for bankruptcy, and he was subsequently laid off, none of us were particularly surprised. As usual, the news hyped it up and made it seem like a big shock. Bankers were flabbergasted, and traders seemed to be utterly powerless to the loss in their portfolios, but to those of us with a roommate on the inside, we had already expected it.

In business school, I learned of countless other similar stories, the most notable and infamous of which would be Enron. Once the golden child of Wall Street, it's now only spoken of as a cautionary tale when teaching young accountants to illustrate what not to do. Having been in high school when the 2008 bubble burst, and later reading and then eventually watching the film *The Big Short*, I became further convinced that businesses do not just fail. Economic bubbles do not just burst. Instead, there are countless warning signs, markers, and alarm bells that go off beforehand, often not only noticed by those close but willingly ignored by many others supposed to regulate and prevent such things.

What I didn't expect but learned about five years into my career was that great, well-meaning people were actually being incentivized to willingly ignore these warning signs. By this point, I had made it to lead consultant. I was officially a subject matter expert, and I had been called in to help an executive team of sellers understand how we could help a client spend a chunk of their money.

In preparation for the meeting, I had spent the last few weeks learning all I could about the new client and their business. Suffice it to say I didn't even think they needed me or the tech I was an expert in, but since my opinion would cost my company half a million dollars in revenue in that year alone, not to mention countless more since most technology sales are renewed year after year, a lot of people wanted to discuss my viewpoint at length.

Kiera, my boss, was also on the call. The seven other people on the phone were all vice presidents, each owning some facet of the surrounding business we were discussing. As I wrapped up my analysis, I paused to allow for questions. What happened next was not only unexpected but something I had never experienced before. As I asked if anyone had any comments or questions, only one man spoke up. He was blunt, and he wasted no time with niceties. His words chilled me to my very core. He said, "Just one comment; you are wrong."

At this point, I was at a loss for words. I had said nothing that everyone I worked with hadn't been saying for months. With the coming changes from Google, the biggest player in the industry, everyone was now saying the same thing. The present technology my team and I focused on was going away. It was very rapidly becoming obsolete. Everyone was saying it was going to die, and everyone was saying it was getting replaced with something newer.

Up to this point, I had never had anyone, much less a Vice President, say, "You're wrong."

That's not to say I haven't been wrong; I have. I'm human, and time changes all things. However, being this blunt and this confident about a directly conflicting opinion, especially opposing my expertise in my own subject matter, was new. Even when people disagreed, they didn't respond in terms of me being right or wrong. Instead, they would steer me in another direction or use lingo like *"I hear what you're saying, but have you considered this?"* Or they would just jump in and start asking questions. Occasionally, I got a few folks who would point out we were talking about two different things. But never had someone been so blunt about me being wrong. To make matters worse, besides my boss, I didn't really know anyone else on the call very well.

The tech industry being what it is, with its flexible schedules and remote working conveniences, attracts and allows people from all walks of life all across the world to now work together remotely. As such, it wasn't uncommon to hear three or four different accents during a single thirty-minute meeting. This one was no exception. Kiera was from Chicago. I was from Denver. There was Arjun, an American-born Indian man working out of San Francisco. Kenny, the VP of Sales in charge of closing the new business, was from Africa. Finally, there was Lee, the VP of our Preference Management engagement, who was calling in from Atlanta and was the same man who had just said I was wrong.

After the call ended, those words continued to ring in my ears— *you're wrong, you're wrong—you're wrong.* Naturally, I began to gaslight and question myself.

Had I missed something? Did I misspeak? Did I say one thing, but it sounded like another? Did I need to find a better way to say what I wanted? Could people without my domain expertise even understand me? In recent years, I learned that getting expertise was relatively easy. More or less, it required repeatedly showing up daily and spending focused time exploring and studying, often digging in when new questions arose naturally. In essence, expertise was a simple equation of time spent plus focused attention. However, in this particular instance, the more time I spent thinking, the more I produced questions instead of answers.

During times like this, it is all too tempting to slink back, hide, and assume someone else knows better. I have seen many people stunt their careers, or in the case of my college roommate, watch idly as the business begins and then continues to fail all around them. Of course, it's possible that we do this because we learned something, maybe unintentionally, from our days back in school. Rather than question the teacher, push back, or make a direct argument against the prevailing opinion or thought track of the majority, we go along, ignoring and, in some cases, purposely suppressing our inner questions, doubts, and curiosities in order to accept or simply stomach the popular and widely accepted views of those all around us.

Or, maybe such a decision is made altruistically, in an attempt to not be difficult, rude, or make the other person look like a fool in front of their peers. It's also possible we do this out of laziness. Knowing, arguing, or bringing up a directly conflicting point will cause the meeting discussion to last longer, ultimately preventing us from making it to happy hour on time. Maybe we simply stay quiet because we know the odds are very high that there is always going to be another meeting or phone call about it anyway.

Or maybe the reason we slink back, hide, and keep our opinions to ourselves is because we know, for whatever reason, our opinions won't matter anyway. Rather than running a risk and speaking up, we simply save our opinion for our spouse, friend, or roommate. Talk with enough people, and it doesn't take very long to find someone who works with stupid people, has a greedy boss, or is surrounded by stupid corporate rules.

Either way, all of these justifications result in the same outcome. A general sense of helplessness that eventually leads to a total lack of personal accountability. In other words, we conclude that everything going wrong in our environment is someone else's problem. After all, how much motivation does one have to stop a business from failing or question/argue with someone who outranks them if they have already accepted it's beyond their power, responsibility, or ability to do so?

Throughout my career, I found that some of the biggest and best moves I ever made were bold. More often than not, they were the one thing that scared me the most. If you want to make more money while working less, you have to be bold. You have to share what you do know, and you have to question others when they share things you don't. In other words, you have to participate even when you're scared it will make you look stupid or uninformed.

After gaslighting myself for a few minutes and finding only more questions than answers, I did what most people today would find to be unthinkable. I called him. At this point in my career, I was thirsty to learn everything I could about everything I could. So, when Lee directly disagreed with me, and I couldn't quickly figure out why, I knew the fastest way to an answer was to get it from the same man who started the whole thing in the first place.

Me, "Hey Lee, it's Sean McMann. You know, I'll admit, that's a first for me. I've never had someone tell me I'm blatantly wrong, much less when I know I'm not. I'm curious what you see that I don't. What am I missing?"

I then paused and waited for him to carry the conversation forward. Throughout my life, I have found it best to leverage silence in times like this—times of confusion, high stress, anxiety, and fear. This little, albeit unbelievably uncomfortable, hack has been a career game-changer. Correctly leveraged silence avoids appearing nervous or inexperienced by rambling, over-apologizing, or sharing too much. At exactly the same time, it naturally conveys a sort of calm and natural confidence all top performers need to get ahead.

Lee, a professional, hardworking, brilliant black man from Atlanta, didn't respond angrily. Like me, he wasn't a bully. Instead, he laughed.

Lee, "Sean, I'm glad you called. The industry is moving away from the tech; it's not that I thought you were wrong; it's that I disagreed with the idea that the client even needed it. The tech isn't going away; it's just that something else is now in vogue and is selling as better and cheaper."

Whatever your go-to justification is, it's safe to say that situations like this one, where someone directly disagrees with you or says something you directly disagree with, are stressful. Add the fact you never really learned how to deal with conflict since it's not like you attended twelve-plus years of *conflict resolution* right after math class, and it's easy to see why such a situation would utterly knock you off balance.

Too often, I think we allow these feelings to silence and hold us back. We hypothesize that someone like Lee must know something we don't. So, we slink back and remain silent, assuming that the reason folks like Lee get promoted instead of us is because they have more information, are smarter, or are just more willing to do what we're not.

In my experience, however, this couldn't be further from the truth. The reason folks like Lee get promoted is not because they have more information but because they are more willing to act on the information they do have. They care more about the result, about making sure the decision being made is arguably the right one, instead of the one most presently agreeable and easily found. Most importantly, don't assume doing nothing is ever the right call. As I learned in college, doing nothing surely results in businesses failing.

End of Chapter Exercise:

1. The next time fear sends you into a gaslighting anxiety thought spiral, pick up the phone and call the person you fear. Most of the time, people are more kind over the phone than email anyway. If they are rude—who cares. Be proud you had the guts to make a call. They likely have some childhood trauma they haven't resolved. Remember that the majority of people let an unknown number go to voicemail. So, before you call, spend two minutes planning a quick voicemail for them to call you back. If it helps, you can always remember the quote, "Those who matter don't mind, and those who mind don't matter."
2. Whether they work with you or you work for them, most people want everyone around them to do the best job possible. So, when you call, make sure you explain you want to learn or understand what they meant. Everyone, just like you, appreciates an opportunity to explain what they think and why.

Chapter 13 | Complainers Not Needed

"People do not seem to realize that their opinion of the world is also a confession of character." - Ralph Waldo Emerson

A FRIEND OF MINE WOULD REGULARLY VOICE HER FRUSTRATION that her career had been stunted because her boss regularly didn't give her the recognition or credit she deserved. To my dismay, she often did this at work functions. Expanding on it for anyone who would listen, she would back up her claims with valid evidence that others had even received credit for her work. She also had countless examples of great opportunities given to others when she was clearly the most qualified for the job.

I often meet people just like her, who think the problem is a lack of opportunity or permission from their boss. Now, obviously, there is no doubt that those given more opportunities throughout their life are more likely to, at least eventually, succeed at one. But complaining about someone else's good fortune not only annoys most people but can convey a level of immaturity you do not want as part of your reputation. Throughout my own career, I've learned that opportunities are everywhere, and waiting for a boss to hand you one is not only dumb but a surefire way to get labeled as a complainer instead of a top performer.

Although it's all too tempting to think the problem is a lack of opportunity from your boss, the real problem is thinking you need one handed to you or that you need permission to seize the one right in front of you.

Fortunately for both of us, I had a mentor who taught me this very early on in my career. If you had met Isabel and me back then, I can guarantee one thing: you would have remembered us. She was brilliant

Complainers Not Needed

and fearless, and after working with her for eight months, I could clearly see why she had such a great reputation for closing new business. In meetings, she was never shy. If she had questions, you knew it. If our boss asked us to do something that didn't serve her immediate goal, she'd let me handle it. When it came to prioritizing her attention, she was a Jedi master.

Occasionally, our teammates would get annoyed or roll their eyes when she would ask dumb questions. She always pretended not to notice. She was seemingly too focused on winning. She didn't appear scared of anything, and it definitely didn't take long for me to see that she didn't care what others thought of her. No one seemed to make her nervous, no matter what their title was. As a mentor, she would regularly ask me to do things that, had I more time to think about, would have scared the shit out of me, paralyzing me and my career trajectory.

Fortunately, she was so determined to win she didn't care what my role was supposed to be. I was talking directly with leaders, product owners, or anyone we needed answers from. We didn't ask permission; instead, we went where we needed to, knowing full well we'd likely need to apologize and ask for forgiveness later. My other new grad colleagues were doing assistant-like work or serving as arm candy in front of clients.

I was given an objective and told to hit it. If I failed, she'd explain how she would have handled it. She'd talk me through the underlying strategy, and to her brilliance, she would then push me back into the corporate jungle to try again. As my new grad colleagues were getting the guts to ask for more challenging and stimulating work, I was already honing my instincts and learning what needed to happen. Unlike what I learned in school, I was learning through failure instead of avoiding it at all costs.

In my first few weeks under Isabel, I quickly learned, contrary to popular belief, that failing is the single fastest way to learn. Additionally, I learned that most supervisors saw it as their job to ensure you didn't fail instead of picking you up, dusting you off, and giving you the confidence to try again when you did.

If you struggle to find an opportunity worth seizing, start with the following steps:

1. Talk to those all around you, including the supervisor's supervising supervisors. Ask them where they see the most opportunity and expected growth.
2. More often than not, opportunities with the potential to provide both career advancement and a raise exist in plain sight, often hidden under the guise of boring endeavors, annoying but mandatory requirements, or fully explored solutions. Sometimes, they simply exist in the thing that is no longer currently in vogue.
3. Commit to one of the opportunities you feel good about. View it as a bet instead of a decision that will make or break your career.
4. Accept that most people go where the crowd says they should. So don't be dismayed if you are seemingly the odd duck out when you bet a few months or a few years of your career on an opportunity no one else is willing to.
5. Don't get distracted or discouraged, and like my friend, let others' success in the most popular or loudest opportunities discourage you. We all can provide value, and we all can help contribute in our own unique way.

Using the steps above has led me to capitalize on the biggest opportunity of my career. After working for Isabel, I began working for a man named Bryan. He had launched a division seven years earlier that was effectively in charge of two solutions. One was a partner solution that we sold on their behalf and managed for our joint clients. The other solution was completely ours, built by our developers and homegrown in-house.

At the time, everyone wanted to be on the partner solution, which made sense since, for all intents and purposes, it was clearly the sexier and more visible opportunity. For one, everyone seemed to want to hear about it, which created a sense of demand and prestige not experienced anywhere else on our team. The other didn't receive nearly as much attention but had a very healthy annually recurring client base while maintaining a relatively low level of ongoing effort.

Admittedly, I, like everyone, was initially drawn to the more popular and sexier partner solution. Fortunately for me, one night on the road, I had a conversation with Bryan that changed my focus, allowing me to find the largest opportunity of my career. One that had been right in front of me the whole time. Over dinner, I asked Bryan where he had seen the most opportunities on our team. He admitted that he thought our homegrown solution was the better overall business. The margins were better, and the constant developments we were making on the product were only going to increase them. Furthermore, clients came back year after year with an almost perfect 100 percent renewal rate. On the other hand, the sexier partner solution not only had far smaller margins but often got in-housed by our clients, typically only after the first year or two.

With all the travel, effort, and time spent not only taking care of the clients but initially closing the deal and then staying apprised of updates and recent communications with our partner, we practically made no money at all. Add the fact most clients in-housed the solution by often poaching our people, and it was easy to argue that we actually lost money in the long run.

No matter how many opportunities you see your boss give to others, there is always another one waiting for you. It's simply a matter of finding it. Sometimes, they are hidden in plain sight, and sometimes, you will need to deploy the tactics explained in Part 3, Chapter 1, *The Fastest Way to More $$$*. Either way, complaining about the behavior of others is surely a waste of time.

End of Chapter Action Items:

1. Talk to others. Ask your colleagues, clients, friends, or others in your industry where they see the most opportunity.
2. Start to compile a list. It's easier to avoid complaining about how unfair things are when you can easily reference countless other ways to realize success.
3. Fortune favors the brave, so make a bet and then jump into it head-on. Set a reminder on your calendar for three, six, or nine months out to check your progress and reevaluate if it's paying off. Even if your first few bets don't make you fabulously wealthy, the additional learnings will increase your chances of further success later on. Remember, knowledge is power.

Part 4: Hacking to Actually Like Your Life

Chapter 14 | Going for Gold

"Never take advice from people who aren't where you want to be."
- Jake Downey

IT'S GENERALLY ASSUMED THAT WORKING LESS AND MAKING MORE will surely make anyone happier, almost like happiness is the end result of a tidy and simple math problem. On the one hand, there are the hours you're no longer working combined with the added money you're now making. On the other, is the supposed automatic end result, ultimate and everlasting happiness.

To my surprise, as my income increased by $154K, this assumption and the logic it's rooted in did not work. Instead of finding everlasting happiness or even, at a minimum, an increased amount comparable to $154K, I found myself more miserable than ever before. As I experienced firsthand and directly contrary to popular belief, becoming professionally and financially successful was not a guaranteed solution to finding happiness. Instead, what I found true both for myself and the countless others like me was that now, we just all had more to lose. Rather than financial success liberating us to follow our dreams and contribute even more to society, it instead introduced an entirely new form of constraint, further imprisoning us in our lives and current careers.

As time kept ticking, I started realizing I was confused. Slowly, that confusion began morphing into a seething frustration that grew into a depression and then a very real sense of self-loathing and hopelessness. As this became more apparent to all those around me, a deluge of other successful people came to my aid. Through this aid, I began to see the all too familiar ways people hid their true feelings from themselves.

These people explained what worked for them. Their solutions included things like going to therapy, playing more golf, taking longer vacations, or, in some cases, drinking more. Others bought bigger houses, fancier cars, or in a few rare instances, even found themselves a mistress or two. No matter how seemingly different the suggestions were, the underlying solution always had the same thing in common. Spend more money. Use external validation and nice things to stave off or completely hide the unpleasant feelings inside. If consumerism were a religious cult, this might be its core creed. In effect, use material things or lavish experiences to reassure you of your success instead of listening to how you feel or what decisions you wish you would have made instead.

Admittedly, such a strategy worked well enough when I was younger, and at times when it invariably didn't, there was always something readily available to drink or smoke to the point I hardly noticed it wasn't working anymore. That said, now with two kids of my own, I shuddered at the idea that they, too, would feel this way if their lives became successful. Having studied Greek philosophy, stoicism, and Buddhism throughout my twenties, I already knew that the problem I was wrestling with was unsolvable through these old, shallow, and consumerist methods. First, thinking my unhappiness was rooted in addiction, I stopped drinking and smoking, ultimately moving toward a healthier lifestyle. To my surprise, the feelings still remained, but my social group didn't.

Unintentionally, my sobriety introduced a riff and point of separation into my relationships with all those around me since part of what we all had in common were the same habits that my sobriety removed. Now, on the hunt for a solution to my feelings and a new friend group, I found people everywhere who felt just like I did. By definition, they are financially successful yet trapped and utterly powerless when it comes to actually changing their lives for the better. Particularly common among these people was their complete acceptance of this just being how things worked.

One man I spoke with put it particularly well. A partner at a prestigious law firm, he shared that regularly, people approached him asking for his advice. They would gush about how he had the dream and how they longed to get it themselves. All the while, he confided in me that he woke up every day wondering how the hell he got where he was. Although others saw it as a dream, it seemed more to him like a sort of nightmare. A mild one for sure, but still one he'd like to change.

Upon asking if he was happy, he paused, laughed, and then answered, "No, but I live an expensive lifestyle; this is the price for it." If spending more and more money to seek external validation is consumerism's core creed, then having to achieve your professional dreams before finally realizing they are not what you actually wanted in the first place is simultaneously its biggest flaw and best-kept secret. Assuming it's more common than we realize, finally getting there and then feeling too trapped to pivot or change course is the biggest economic tragedy of our time.

During the years that I spent working on this book, a theory about happiness and its link to fulfillment emerged. Although not perfect, it was surprisingly different than the one practiced by families everywhere. If summarized into a formula, it involved maximizing personal fulfillment through following one's intuition instead of minimizing the time worked in a respectable and high-paying profession. The idea that happiness was not an easily copied and pasted formula espoused by those who claimed it publicly, but a sort of Eldorado only found by listening to one's own intuition and inner voice, wasn't a secret per se, but more an intentionally ignored fact of life.

If you've made it to this point in the book, you have undoubtedly started focusing on the one or two aspects of your work that really matter. You have effectively rearranged your day to do those things first, thereby becoming more effective while simultaneously setting yourself up to work less. You have evaluated your company and your current career position to outline a few of the ways you could make more money in a fraction of the time when compared to waiting for a traditional raise. Following the insight from the last chapter, you have also drafted a unique list of opportunities all around you that can be explored and bet on to further increase your chances of continuing to make more. In effect, you are now well on your way to earning more while working less. The problem that no one else will tell you is that what you actually wanted had nothing to do with either of these things in the first place.

Assuming you're like most and have spent the majority of your life going to school and then work, both essentially adhering to schedules

Going for Gold

made by others, expecting you to suddenly know how to create your own while simultaneously being completely confident and comfortable that it leads to your personal fulfillment would be ridiculous. Regardless of whether they are good or bad, habits, once formed, are incredibly hard to break. In today's society, work and its surrounding schedule are arguably the biggest habits of our day-to-day lives.

It probably doesn't help that countless self-help gurus out there today promise that finding work-life balance, a sort of equilibrium between how much you work and how much you make, will surely produce happiness. Besides my personal experience to the contrary, I also couldn't find any evidence that making the most amount of money for the least amount of work was good for you, let alone sustainable for our society. Even more surprising was the fact I couldn't find a single book that explained how and when to turn off or skip said habits.

These realizations are what led me, to the dismay of my editor, to significantly change and rewrite the last part of this book in its final hour. Rather than only addressing the hacks and habits that made my career the most successful, I realized a better book would need to include the habits that led to me feeling the most fulfilled. The same habits simultaneously produced an internal conflict that, at the time, made me wildly uncomfortable but, maybe coincidentally, also more valuable. The same habits, at least for a little while, led me to no longer feeling trapped.

Since you were taught all your life to work forty or more hours a week, working less and making more is surely going to cause you some mental discomfort. Knowing this, the habits provided in this last section of the book will serve, first, as an intermediary step to help you avoid insanity as you begin working less. In the long term, they will also serve as a doorway, enabling you to find those elusive things that produce personal fulfillment and ultimate life enjoyment. These are things that are both incredibly personal and almost entirely extinct in today's corporate jungle.

Although happiness might not work like an algebraic math problem, I do think our lives might. The end result is the sum total of everything you add up. Sometimes, the math works out as we'd expect. Other times, we don't notice we focus on the wrong variables until we get to the end. I think at least one of the big reasons for this is that, in the end, we can't hide anything anymore. We can't pretend the added combination of our alcoholism and lack of community involvement were choices we had no choice to make. As we age, using bills to justify the fact we missed out on our children's childhood seems, at least in part, to lose its validity. So, take it from me: although the preceding habits might take time and require a certain level of grit, they are undoubtedly worth it because you and your life are too.

End of Chapter Action Items:

1. Look at your calendar for the past week. What did you do for yourself? Of all the items on there, what can be considered self care? Things like going to therapy, yoga, running, or any other form of exercise you enjoy. If you're a sports fan, how many games did you go to last week? How many nights did you stretch? How many morning did you wake up and drink 12 oz of water before anything else?
2. Write that number down. If you're like most, the majority of your life is spent helping to care for the economy while ensuring you don't end up homeless. Don't be discouraged if its low, or even zero. Before I began the journey that would eventually have me write this book, my number was zero and my version of self care was simply over eating and watching too much television.
3. Start where you are today, and take it one day, one step at a time.

Chapter 15 | Thirty Minutes for Fulfillment

"It is no measure of health to be well adjusted to a profoundly sick society."
- Jiddu Krishnamurti

A LONG TIME AGO, I HEARD A STORY ABOUT A DOCTOR AND HIS SON. Truth be told, I have no idea if it's true, but like all fables, I think its inherent lesson is worth retelling. Like most fathers who want a good life for their children, this one encouraged him to follow in his footsteps and also become a doctor. Not wanting to disappoint his father, the son obliged. He worked hard, went to a top-tier medical school, and eventually, like his father, became a doctor.

Years later, now retired, the father confided in his son over a cup of coffee one Sunday that he never actually wanted to be a doctor. He, instead, wanted to be a teacher. But his father, our young doctor's grandfather, having been a teacher all his life, encouraged his son to instead be a doctor. Knowing doctors commanded more respect and made far more money. Our young doctor, almost in tears, now wished, more than anything, that he had the courage to tell his father years ago that he, too, dreamed of being a teacher.

As I get older, I'm always jealous of those people who knew from an early age what they wanted to be when they grew up. Having spent most of my life making things up as I go along, I often wonder if I would have felt significantly more fulfilled had I known early on what I wanted to do. Although my parents never told me to become a doctor, I was directly encouraged not to become a teacher. Like our young doctor, I arrived at my first career largely by combining what those all around me told me to do or, in some instances, what not to do with what was readily available.

Yet at some point, as my career continued progressing, it occurred to me that if I kept doing what everyone around me told me to, then I couldn't expect to make any more than everyone else. After all, if everyone else was doing the same thing, too, why would any sensible human being pay me more for it? Most of us think that if we follow our boss's direction, do a good job meeting expectations, and then put in enough hours, we'll eventually be promoted. This is the same line of thought that leads us to believe working a good job, one that others told us to, would lead us to feeling fulfilled.

However, if I had learned anything from working under Isabel, it was that top performers were always different. They asked questions when others didn't, they read things others wouldn't even bother with, and they formed their own opinions instead of simply believing the opinion of the majority. Most of all, they all achieved success and found fulfillment by going their own unique way.

Going your own, unique way, at first blush, sounds heroic and charming until it comes time to do it. After all, we all have bills and, in some instances, bills of others, and going our own way, although generally the backbone of any great movie, is not so easily enacted when our livelihoods are on the line. This possibly explains why any promising, intelligent young man who wanted to be a teacher would instead become a doctor.

As if finding one's own unique way wasn't hard enough, it's very possible that you like me, have never done it before. Although I had believed myself to be a rebel without a cause most of my life, most of the decisions I had made up until that point provided more the illusion of choice than any actual choice. After all, all the sports I could play throughout my childhood were already approved by the school board governing where I attended. The classes I took were usually some combination of a finite number of choices some dean thought would work in preparing me for the next level. The food I ate was usually approved by the state, my parents, or both, and the friends I hung out with were, in large part, the result of the careful family planning and neighborhood hunting my parents had enacted when I was younger. In short, my life was the story of any suburban kid. It was, as any modern housing development brochure reads today, architected and full of all the things any child needs to be successful.

That said, if you manage your career like my childhood, you are not

Thirty Minutes for Fulfillment

going to be very different from the millions of other kids who also grew up in the burbs. Meaning you are very likely not going to be worth any more money than any of them either. To differentiate yourself, you need to seek out the advice and guidance of someone who has what you want. They could have a fancy title, a cool sports car, or any of the other traditional objects you have equated to mean success. For me, at that point in my life, it wasn't only material objects I was after. It was also a certain skill level.

Based on all the evidence, listening to your dad about what job to take or how to appease your boss might be a good thing. I say might because it seems that would very much depend on who your dad is, and what he's accomplished. More importantly, if his accomplishments are ones you want for yourself.

Wanting, like so many of us, to be better or even, dare I say, the best, I turned to the best performer I could find. In four short years, Isabel had gone from inheriting a book of accounts worth $350K to running the largest in our entire division, now worth $6.5 million. If anyone was going to be able to help teach me how to be the best, it would be her.

After taking weeks trying to build up enough courage, I finally bit the bullet and asked her to teach me. When I did, her response didn't match anything I had heard in college, nor anything I had heard before or since in the corporate jungle. She didn't say it would come with time, or you must make senior associate first. She didn't say get a master's degree. Above all else, she certainly didn't cite some dumb corporate structure, employee handbook, or obscure rule. She also didn't cite some shadowy, Oz-like executive as a valid reason why she couldn't teach me.

Instead, she said, "It's easy," and then gave me a book.

Upon handing me the book, she then told me which chapters mattered and which ones didn't—which ones I could skip because I already knew the information or which ones I'd have to learn by trial and error. Convinced that this book was my map through the corporate jungle to untold riches and career success, I became in a word—obsessed. The first week was relatively easy, but as time passed, the amount of dedication, faith, focus, and conviction needed to keep going only seemed to increase.

The direct connection between how much time I spent reading

and how hard it became, surprisingly, wasn't because of the material itself. Having graduated from business school not two years earlier, I was relatively used to reading dry business books, memos, and other materials. What made it so hard was everything else I missed out on. In order to keep reading that book, I had to skip plenty of internal company training and other gatherings. Sometimes, I even opted to stay home and read instead of going out with friends. During those few months that it took me to read that book, the anxiety I felt was substantial.

I was now clearly deviating from the majority. Worse, as I tried to stay focused, others began getting rewarded. Sometimes, it was a simple 'thank you' exchanged from a leader to a colleague who had attended the meeting I missed. Other times, it was an actual promotion. As the list of items I had missed out on grew, so too did my doubts. It wasn't long before I began wondering if I was making the right decision. Maybe I had placed too much confidence in Isabel. Maybe I should stop and go back to doing what everyone else was doing. Maybe I should do it soon before it was too late and inevitably ruined my career.

Fortunately for me, two things regularly occurred that allowed me to continually ignore such thoughts. First, Isabel would periodically check-in and ask me how it was going without warning. She'd ask what chapter I was on, what insights I was gleaming from the text, and if I had any questions. With our trust in one another growing by the day, I began asking for opportunities to apply some of the lessons. Not all were feasible or immediately available, but the sheer prospect of even one being possible made the material that much more interesting.

In hindsight, my questions must have also instilled a level of faith in Isabel, indirectly communicating my intelligence and growing understanding of the material. As time went on, she began giving me more opportunities to succeed. She also began inviting me to meetings way above my pay grade for the sheer sake of my learning. Afterward, we'd debrief, and then she'd often assign me part of the work. Over time, I began doing parts of her job, setting me up to eventually receive two promotions in two and a half years.

The second ongoing thing that helped keep me engaged in the book Isabel recommended was the daily ritual I set up around it. Each day, before opening an email or checking in with my boss, I'd sit down at my desk with a fresh cup of coffee and read. Still young and nervous that someone would yell at me for slacking off, I'd set a timer for twenty-five minutes and then allow myself to get lost in the material. My reasoning was that anyone could disappear for twenty-five minutes without hardly being noticed. After all, that was just like taking two bathroom breaks at once. Once the timer went off, I'd refill my cup of coffee and get back to doing whatever I was supposed to be doing. Before letting the stress of work and daily life invade my brain, I filled it with the new information Isabel recommended.

To my surprise and eventual delight, this habit led me to begin looking forward to starting my day at work. Rather than arriving and dreading the countless emails I had to write, I began anticipating my cup of coffee and twenty-five minutes of learning. After having kids, the pleasure I derived from this time each day only grew. It was almost like I got a twenty-five-minute break to learn and read in between my dad job and my paying one. As time went on, the amount I was able to learn grew beyond anything I had ever anticipated. To see the summarized version of the full list, please see Appendix A at the back of the book.

Unfortunately, we often put our development, learning, and self-improvement at the bottom of our daily to-do lists. A real tragedy knowing the more we learn, the more we'll be worth, and the more opportunities that will come our way. At first, I only focused on reading the book that Isabel gave me. Over time, I took on countless other topics based on what drew my curiosity. Sometimes, I spent my time progressing in an online coding class; other times, I would spend those minutes trying to debug a browser I was building. As my career and responsibility grew, I eventually took on subjects like negotiation, corporate law, machine learning, venture capital, private equity, and countless other topics.

After months of working on a particularly technical, dense, or hard subject, I'd switch to reading a biography about a successful CEO, politician, or other prominent historical figure. These served not only as sources of great inspiration but also as a more entertaining reprieve when my mind needed something less intense while still being wholly educational.

I'm told that as a child, I loved to talk. To this very day, my mom still remembers the first teacher I ever had that didn't complain about how much I did. If you're curious, I was in the fourth grade, and his name was

Thirty Minutes for Fulfillment

Mr. Sautel. In any event, my ability to talk, coupled with my continually growing knowledge base, began shifting my career in a whole different direction. Eventually, I found myself perfectly positioned for a unique role I wanted instead of fighting for the next promotion everyone else was competing for. Additionally, my conversations with clients and leaders alike started to change. Eventually, Isabel wasn't the only one they found interesting.

As my contributions started to get bigger and make larger impacts, so too did my raises. Alongside it, my confidence grew, and so did my personal fulfillment. I began leaving work feeling proud of what I had accomplished, could accomplish, and would accomplish tomorrow. Being able to talk about a lot of subjects in depth also increased my self-confidence. I began speaking up more in meetings, more confident that the questions I asked were informed and good. As such, executives, team leaders, and other prominent figures in the firm started knowing who I was by name, which is an absolute necessity if you want to keep rising in an organization. After all, as silly as it sounds, you can't get promoted to a position of influence if no one knows who you are.

Now, we'll get to the protocol itself in a minute. Before we do, let's discuss the single biggest objection most people have to such a daily habit: time. I'm sure a few of you are already thinking—*oh, I wish I could spare twenty-five minutes a day, but who has the time? I'm just so busy. You don't understand, my work is different*—blah blah blah.

My response? Bullshit! I don't buy that you're too busy.

If you're like most people, you spend way more time watching TV, texting, sending memes to friends, or aimlessly scrolling on Instagram or TikTok. Imagine for a moment if you simply used twenty-five minutes of that time every day to invest in yourself. What could that do for you and your career in a month, a year, or over a decade? What about over your lifetime? If you shoot for five days a week and only hit three, completing twenty-five minutes of daily learning. That accounts for 600 hours of learning over the next ten years. If you hit five days a week, you'll have completed 10,000 hours in that same time frame.

Maybe your objection isn't about time. Maybe it's about your reputation and your moral code. Some of you, after all, might argue that spending twenty-five minutes reading or learning something new while on your employer's dime is stealing. That is a very understandable argument, especially if you're paid hourly. But, by that logic, the minute they ask you to do more, wouldn't they be stealing from you?

What about the minute they call and ask you to cover for someone who called in sick? Even if you say no, most companies don't pay you for the minute or two you spent answering the phone or responding to a text. Furthermore, no employer is going to promote or reward employees who remain static. In today's economy, employers practically demand innovation, adaptation, and growth. Unfortunately, they just don't always know how to practice encouraging it in their people.

Times change and people change, and contrary to popular belief, executives don't actually control the flow of money in their firm long term. Instead, customers and investors do. So, if your role, and thereby your boss, really don't expect you to evolve, then at a very minimum, you should realize it's only a matter of time before you are replaced by a machine because regardless of who your boss is, or what they believe, the investors and consumers of today expect it.

Now that you have waited long enough, I'm finally going to walk you through the step-by-step guide to this daily habit. One that will surely supercharge your career and help you navigate the ever-complex and changing world of the information economy. The protocol will not only allow you to continue growing, changing, and adapting to our ever-changing economy, but it will simultaneously increase your brain's neuroplasticity. Which scientists define as your brain's ability to change its physical structure and functions in response to its environment. In other words, the more you learn, the more your brain will adapt to make learning easier.

The Thirty Minutes of Mastery Step-by-Step Guide

Step 1: Identify the time of the day you're sharpest, most alert, and most capable. For most people, typically, this time is an hour or two after they wake up. For others, it's right after lunch. Whenever it is, try to block this slot off your calendar as many days a week as possible. For superstar results, do this on the weekends, too. Although twenty-five to thirty minutes is all you'll need, our brains can usually provide one and a half to three hours of focused time between each sleep cycle. As with anything, you'll be much more successful if you plan a little and start on the right foot.

Step 2: Once you find a beautiful timeslot, block thirty minutes of it every day for your thirty minutes of mastery. I recommend limiting your blocking to only one week at a time since kids have emergencies, bosses move up deadlines, and mothers sometimes call. Block it by putting a recurring meeting between you and yourself on your calendar. You'll do this every day for the length of your career, but booking a week at a time often allows for some necessary flexibility as life changes, clients' schedules change, and unanticipated events happen.

Step 3: This is the hard one. Show up and put in the time. Every day, or at a minimum, three days a week. Don't allow distractions or fake emergencies to cancel this time. Don't allow the fact that Monday was a holiday to give you an excuse to skip your Tuesday slot. And never give up this slot to answer emails or respond to friends' texts. The last thing you want is to be worrying about how you're going to respond to your boss or how you'll professionally respond to that upset client while you're trying to learn the basics of robotics, graphics design, manifestation, a coding language, how to be more creative, or whatever else you want to learn. Some folks like to learn subjects outside their immediate profession and expertise; some like to specialize in their immediate area—either work. The goal is for you to learn something, anything. By doing so regularly, you'll be facilitating the creation of new neural connections, enabling increased neuroplasticity in your brain, and improving your ability to think, adapt, and drive value over the length of your life. By investing in yourself for thirty minutes daily, you'll be growing your career while you also grow your brain.

Step 4: Observe yourself honestly and hone your practice. As Annie Dillard said, "How we spend our days is, of course, how we spend our lives." By prioritizing yourself and your daily learning, you will be making an investment in yourself that will pay huge dividends in the long term.

Step 5: Iterate and improve. After your first week, ask yourself: Am I spending thirty minutes daily on this, or is it twenty minutes because I'm not online right at 8 a.m.? Does someone (like your mom) always text you at 8:20 to ensure I made it in safe? If you're brave enough, block your mom's calls during that slot, or don't look at your phone until after 9. Your goal is to lose yourself in whatever you're learning.

Scheduling and spending thirty minutes daily learning is only half of the equation. The other half is quality, focused execution. You don't get points for simply scheduling it and doing your best. As we covered in Part 2, Chapter 1, your goal, like all top performers, is to get into the flow state. So set a timer, put your phone on Do Not Disturb, place it in your bag, and let yourself get absorbed by an online class, podcast, TedTalk, or certification you know will improve your career. I personally have used Udacity, FreeCode Academy, Hoopla (free audiobooks through my local library), and Alison.com (which offers free industry-recognized certifications).

Step 6: Make two lists. The first is a list of things you want to learn more about that interest you. The second is a completed list. Eventually, this list will remind you of everything you've learned and done during this slot. This list will come in handy, as it becomes a source of positive feedback and upliftment to help you keep going on those days you feel off or lose your conviction. As an added bonus, this list will also make it much easier to update your resume periodically.

Although simple, this daily habit will improve your cognitive ability

Thirty Minutes for Fulfillment

while giving you something to look forward to. As this habit builds over time, incredible things happen. For example, by learning code, I started seeing potential solutions and options where only problems existed previously. In one particular scenario, due to an idea I had with a client, we built a solution that worked faster and was precisely what the client wanted. Plus, it even removed some of the things we hated. In other words, our support engineers also enjoyed it and that year was the first in five the client didn't ask for a discount.

As with most things in life, the details matter. During this time every day, stay off your phone! When you're on that phone, you're making someone else money. Not to mention using precious cognitive energy that won't contribute to you getting a raise or eventually working less. When you're learning, creating, doing, or building, you're making yourself money. Even if it's not immediate, the investment is there, and one day it will pay dividends.

Whether you have known what you wanted to do for a living since you were six or whether you're like me and are still not sure, practicing the thirty minutes of mastery every day will allow you to remain competitive in an ever-changing economy. Plus, you might find, like I did all those years ago under Isabel, that such a daily habit also gives you something to look forward to, something that helps you feel fulfilled when the day is done.

Not sure where to start? If years ago, like our young doctor, you chose your profession based on what your dad recommended and instead of what you wanted, start there. For example, investigate what kind of teachers need a medical degree or what kind of doctors are allowed to teach. We no longer live in a world where you have to choose between being a doctor or a teacher. Today, you can be a doctor who teaches or a teacher who is also a doctor. Whatever your passion and wherever your intuition is leading you, follow it. We're all here to contribute and work together in our own unique ways, and the last thing any of us want is to retire wishing we had done something else entirely. No matter how successful society views us, if you spend your life secretly wishing for something else, you might pass on more to your children than you bargained for.

End of Chapter Exercise:

1. Ask yourself, if you could do anything, what would you do? So many times, we erect rules, obstacles, and unfair conditions, brainstorming our own failures before they even happen. Among other things, this has the very real effect of trapping us in our current reality. Realize that no one is trapping you in your job or your life except you.
2. Next, ask yourself what you need to know to do that. Do you need a license, a mentor, or maybe just a connection in the industry? If you're not sure, ask someone who would know.
3. Go on LinkedIn and reach out to someone in that industry or someone already in that profession. See if you can shadow them, take them to coffee, or even have a quick Zoom call to pick their brains and ask for their advice...or like I did, reach out to the person on your team, or across your company that you admire and who appears to have one thing you want. Try your best not to focus on just material things. As I've aged, I've learned most of what I want can't be bought but must be earned and built. When you meet with them, ask them how you could get into the industry. How they did, or how they wish they had. Ask them if they could change one thing about their career, what it would be?
4. Above all else, believe in yourself. Your life can be as adventurous, fun, and fulfilling as it is in your dreams. The first step is just believing it's possible. The next step is to take thirty minutes each day and invest in yourself and that new reality.

Questions to Find What You Want to Learn:

1. If you could be an expert in anything, what would it be?
2. What is something at work that makes you uncomfortable because you don't know enough about it or are insecure about it? Can you learn that or make friends with someone who is already an expert?

Chapter 16 | Landing Another Mentor

"You can never be overdressed or overeducated." - Oscar Wilde

As my time in the corporate jungle continued, I couldn't help but notice a trend. The more supervisors an organization had, the more general paranoia there was that the average worker needed more supervision. At one point, being under six layers of supervisors supervising supervisors, I couldn't help but estimate how much money was being spent on highly paid people whose only job was supervising supervisors of the people actually doing the work. Based on my mental calculations, the answer was tens of millions of dollars, and that was only at my company. To try and imagine the combined number of companies and industries across the world made my head hurt. One day, for fun, I let these thoughts continue until they included all politicians, lobbyists, and governments at large. That day, I got physically ill.

Remain in the corporate jungle long enough, and while observing supervisors supervising supervisors, you might find yourself developing an urge to ask a simple question. Although the question itself is simple, getting the guts to ask it is anything but. The question can be expressed in many ways, but it is generally along the lines of "What do you do all day?" It is usually meant for your boss or someone else higher up on the totem pole who seems to fit the description of a supervisor supervising supervisors.

Most people, of course, never ask such a question. When pressed, they will tell you they know better. Presuming asking such a question would not only make leaders uncomfortable (something many wrongly believe they should never do) but also run the risk of making them look stupid or unintelligent. These same people generally have an issue with any decision made without their consultation and convey the general impression that they always know better. Ironically, they never seem to believe enough in what they know to say anything to those in authority, but that's beside the point.

By now, I hope it's ever apparent to you, dear reader, that I am simply not one of those people. And as it happens, I don't know better. This is what led me to ask such a question of my first C-suite mentor—which brings us to Ken.

Ken had been in a leadership position in our company for the last twenty-plus years, serving the bulk of that tenure as the Chief Operating Officer (COO). When you followed the trail of supervising supervisors, it basically ended with him. Technically, he did report directly to our CEO, but as most people in the corporate jungle know, CEOs are usually more like investment or hedge fund managers than business owners and operators. In other words, Ken was the guy in charge of day-to-day operations.

When I was younger, folks like Ken scared the crap out of me. Their titles, along with their impressive career trajectories, gave me the false illusion that they were special. Anytime they would come to town, my initial instinct would be to hide. My mind would race, searching for any possible excuse to miss a work dinner, team building exercise, or similar sort of activity that occurred after hours where I'd be forced to make conversation. Oftentimes, others would support this fear by talking of the injustice and general unfairness required to expect anyone to report to a work-related event after hours. Although both of these factors easily combine into a very potent justification not to go, the obvious truth is that such a decision will surely stunt your career.

So often, people think that if they work hard, keep their noses to the ground, and plug along, folks like Ken will eventually reward them with a slingshot-like promotion that ushers them into leadership positions. However, this assumption, although logically sound, misses a few things. For one, it completely neglects the fact that those leaders are also people, and like all people, they are more likely to trust those that they already know. It also completely ignores the fact that as a prominent leader, you'd have to regularly talk and chat with those already in charge—the same ones that currently scare the crap out of you.

Landing Another Mentor

Lastly, and probably most important of all, it reveals a complete misunderstanding of what such a leader actually does. This brings us to the question of how one learns such things. Assuming you don't already have a lot of C-suite connections in your network, you'll presumably have to take steps to make them. A goal that will become extraordinarily easier if you already have a general sense of what they do. That's where I can help get you started. If you don't want to be in the C-suite but would rather just understand your boss better or add your name to the hat for the next promotion, this section will help you regardless. As instrumental as Isabell was for both my career and my personal growth, her expertise was focused on selling, not necessarily managing or running a multimillion-dollar business. To learn that, I knew I needed a new mentor.

They say luck is at the intersection of hard work and opportunity. Work hard long enough, and the underlying assumption presumes that a great opportunity will come along. Yet, this school of thought doesn't ever seem to explain how to create that sort of opportunity.

I'll give the reader a hint: it's certainly not by missing get-togethers with leadership because one's dog is sick, the kids are out of school, or because one's husband is out of town. It might sound silly, but the fastest way to get the mentor you want, is to first spend time with them. Probably above all, leaders want to believe that their people care. By using any sort of excuse to miss a meet and greet, no matter how sick the dog really is, you are subtly sending the signal that your dog is more important than the business. No matter how true this might be, it's certainly not the message you want to convey to the guy in charge of said business. After all, it is very likely that he didn't get there by caring more about his dog.

Although working hard and doing all you can to help a business succeed is essential to moving up, you'll never rise as high as you want to if you don't place yourself in the direct path of those able to grant such a promotion.

There is no arguing that deluding yourself into thinking you always know better while using excuses to avoid talking to those who actually do might be a very useful tactic to reassuring yourself how smart you are. It should also come as no surprise that such a strategy is equally effective in ensuring you don't ever get that slingshot promotion.

Landing Another Mentor

During all my time in the corporate jungle, I have never met anyone at the top of their field, whether they were C-suite executives, top-performing salespeople, or prominent and brilliant engineers who didn't constantly and repeatedly seek additional understanding. Of all the top performers I ever worked with, none of them were satisfied in simply accepting what they already knew. Instead, they all shared one quality. A tenacious thirst for more information and a deeper and more holistic understanding.

If you don't already have a rapport with a senior leader or know when they are coming to town next, that's ok. You are in luck since, given the exponential rise in modern technology, there are now more ways than ever to create such an opportunity. The steps to do so are simple but will require time. Contrary to your wildest dreams, slingshot promotions are more the result of years of hard work, networking, asking questions, and being patient than they are some divine act of God. They do not happen overnight, and they certainly don't happen if you stay home every time someone with real power comes to town.

So, to help you in this endeavor, I looked back on all the times I did the bold thing. The times I introduced myself to the CEO or the president of operations when my job was just to field customer phone calls. The times I went to the late-night work function instead of going home and sitting on my couch. I reviewed and studied my journals of when I went left and took a chance instead of going right, staying in line, and doing only what was in my job description. What I found was that each time, I followed a general set of the same steps—the steps that I provide below.

Steps to Create Opportunity, Get a Mentor, or Just Get Noticed

1. Show up. As simple as it sounds, it is by far where most people make the biggest mistake. Using excuses like *my dog is sick, I can't, my kids will be out of school, that's really late, and I don't want to*—yada yada. Or even justify it through a line of thinking like, *why would she care who I am? There are four layers of managers between us. There are so many other more important people for her to meet; why would she care about me?* The fact is,

these are all just excuses for you not to do something that makes you uncomfortable. But by doing it, you might not only open yourself up to more opportunities, but you might also find that you're proud of yourself for doing the hard thing. This is a skill and practice, and if done regularly, it will grow your confidence and your career.

2. Do your homework. Prep. Leaders are more likely to remember who you are if you leave a good impression. And presuming talking to leaders makes you anxious like me, having a plan will help with both of these. If they have written a book, read it. If they are featured at a conference, watch their interview. Generally speaking, it's good to have one business/career-related topic and one hobby or fun topic since even executives don't want to spend all their time working. That said, you're not likely to get promoted to the position you want if the CEO only knows you as the guy he can talk football with. So do your homework, and be prepared to discuss a few other subjects than your favorite running back.

3. Don't bullshit. Successful leaders, above all else, are experts at detecting it. If you don't know, say you don't know, and ask them to explain. Contrary to what that voice in your head is saying, no one expects you to know everything and even bosses like to explain and teach.

4. Follow up. Send a thank you note or email, or even better, set a meeting to discuss some lingering questions you had based on your last conversation. Relationships with leaders are built like all others over time through mutual investment. In the beginning, you might have to put in the majority of effort, but over time, you'll find it will get easier and may even start to balance out.

5. Be genuine. Like our office gossiper, so many times, people falsely believe that leaders simply want their opinions to be agreed with. If you disagree, say it politely and in an informed manner. The leaders that mind you disagreeing don't matter, and those that don't mind are more likely to run a very successful company anyway.

Landing Another Mentor

For me, a key opportunity arose during a game of Top Golf. Earlier in the day, Ken gave a presentation to introduce himself to me and the rest of the team. In it, he explained his hobbies, his highly competitive nature, and his career up until that point. The details of which I won't go into, but suffice it to say, I had learned enough to know we had a few areas of common ground. Knowing we both had highly competitive natures, over a round of drinks, I decided to make my move and challenge him to a game of Top Golf.

Now, the game itself didn't go perfectly, and at one point, I was admittedly a little distracted by a pretty waitress. Nevertheless, during the game, Ken offered me his time. It was innocuous and probably meant more as a gesture of kindness than any sort of serious offer. To anyone else, hearing someone in Ken's position say, "Well, anytime you have questions or want to talk, just reach out," might easily be dismissed as a social nicety or a general result of gentile breeding. However, I had learned from my time working with other mentors that if someone in such a position offers anything, no matter how serious it seems, you take it and don't wait.

As Ken flew home, I immediately sent him my first of many meeting invites for us to talk one-on-one. Knowing how busy and protective such leaders are with their time, I presumed it critical to convey to Ken exactly what I expected to talk about. After all, in addition to his offering, I assumed it would be much harder for him to decline such a meeting if he saw I had very specific things to ask him. Using Rule #2, No Blank Meetings, as described in Chapter 5, I hit send and waited.

Two hours later, as his response came back 'accepted,' I knew the hard part was just beginning. The agenda for the meeting was short and sweet and can easily be duplicated and tweaked for your own purposes. The three parts were all provided in bullet point format and read as follows:

- Introductions
- Q/A
- Goal Review (Ken's goals)

For the first part, I intended to get Ken talking about himself. How had he gotten where he was? Did he like it? How did he view the business, etc.? The second part—the Q/A session—was where I'd do two things: thing one, ask questions related to things he had told me up until that point, demonstrating my ability to listen and showing that my next question was informed, and thing two giving me the opportunity to ask questions that I really wanted answers to like, "What did he do all day?"

Obviously, no one gets to Ken's position without knowing the general rules of polite conversation. Meaning he did ask me to explain my own career trajectory and how I had got to where I was, what I knew, who I knew, what my biggest account was, and what the current things I was actively working on were.

The third part, Goal Review, would, of course, help me understand his job better. Up until this point in my career, I had learned that the higher up you go in an organization, the more goals expand, broaden, and become abstract. For example, a goal of mine at the customer level might be to increase customer retention and grow total contract value. In essence, grow my relationship with my clients so that it eventually made us more money. While Ken might read, "Grow profit margin by 5 percent," his goal, of course, could be accomplished partly by me and others like me, who are all growing our client accounts. But it would likely actually be accomplished through some combination of that plus cutting costs. Whether that meant developing automated systems, eliminating some sort of process redundancy, or the much dreaded but now completely expected annual round of layoffs.

As the meeting came, so too did my anxiety. However, this was not my first conversation with an executive leader, and it certainly wasn't going to be the last. To help calm my nerves, I reminded myself that he, too, was also just a man, another person, just like me, who was trying to do his best. At that, I focused on the topics at hand. As his introduction came to an end, and I had run out of follow-up questions to ask, I proceeded to the heart of what I wanted to discuss. When you have a question like "What do you do all day?" it can be ever tempting to bury it in the end, hoping that by doing so, folks won't see how important it is. However, having already mentored and trained younger professionals myself, I knew this strategy to be generally distasteful. In fact, I had learned through experience that the people who asked the one question they really cared about first were the ones I respected the most.

Knowing full well that it might jeopardize my job but that if it did,

Landing Another Mentor

I wouldn't want it anymore anyway, I let it fire immediately after we were done with introductions.

"Ken, the biggest question I have, and the real reason I set this up, was to ask you this first question, one that I have been racking my brain to figure out: what do you do all day?"

Of course, I had imagined and daydreamed about a multitude of possible, and admittedly even a few far-flung responses, the scariest of which included him firing me right there on the spot. However, no matter how wild any of my previously envisioned scenarios got, they couldn't have prepared me for what he said next.

To my relief, he first laughed. He then got pretty serious and said, "I handle pain."

As I nodded while remaining silent, encouraging him to expand on his initial answer, he continued. The gist of which made me think of a chess game. As he spoke about Doug, his number two, I envisioned the queen. A powerful piece that can demolish anything in its path. If, for whatever reason, it acts carelessly, it can easily demolish through the sacrifice of its own fellow pieces. Ken then explained that although he understood some people got really frustrated with Doug, he understood this individual had immutable strength and purpose. After all, Doug was the guy Ken could give a $50 million target to and know it would be hit.

Up to that point, I maybe much like you had thought that the leaders of any great organization were simply the best at business, sales, building technology, or whatever their domain was. What Ken's short but incredibly insightful answer demonstrated was that they were more often the best at seeing and then handling the core skills of all the other individual players. More often than not, they were patient and more adept at handling conflict than anyone else. Rather than being the top-performing quarterback, they were more like the brilliant and stoic head coach hidden behind the scenes.

Just like a chess master doesn't become the best by being an expert in a single piece, a great C-suite leader doesn't successfully run a large enterprise by simply keeping their nose to the ground and working hard. No, they, like experts in any domain, have to become skilled in the combined interaction of all pieces on the board. In essence, they have to simultaneously see the entire forest while hopelessly trying to

Landing Another Mentor

balance the needs of the individual trees. Above all, they have to have an appreciation for the inherent complexity of the corporate jungle and be willing to regularly accept that they very well might not know better than those all around them.

Throughout my career, I have found that a key component to actually liking your life is being brave, getting out of your comfort zone, and placing yourself on the direct path of important people and opportunities. Ironically, this is also the thing most people don't dare do. As tempting as it is to stay home and explain to yourself, your family, your friends, and anyone else who will listen that you had no choice but to miss it because of whatever emergency popped up, we all know the truth. The truth is that rather than running the risk of failing, embarrassing yourself, or being told no, you opted to run away. Instead of taking your shot, you made an excuse as to why you couldn't. Instead of running the risk and maybe hearing something you didn't like or being made to realize you were misinformed, you avoided the situation altogether. Instead of asking the one question you really want to of the one person no one else would dare, you made excuses.

In all my conversations with Ken and others like him, I learned that leaders at the top, above all, don't let fear keep them from being in the room, at the bar, or flying to the conference. They show up, speak their mind, and are brave when others aren't. They handle pain when others think their job shouldn't have any at all. They deal with conflicting opinions when most delude themselves into thinking there is only one right answer. Rather than watching the sea of supervisors supervising supervisors and bitching about the obvious idiocy, they set a meeting with one to find answers.

The truth is, you won't ever like your life if you don't like your career, and you can't like your career if you make excuses instead of asking questions and seeking answers. Whether you thought of a C-suite executive, a division manager, or even your immediate boss while reading this chapter, I have no doubt you have questions you want to ask that up until today, you wouldn't dare. Today, I invite you to dare. Ask the question others won't. Be bold because I guarantee you if the boss hasn't already thought of it, but you and others like you are, they probably should be, and you can be the one to help get them there.

End of Chapter Exercise:

1. Just like Serena Williams, Tiger Woods, Elon Musk or anyone else who has ever achieved anything great, they all started by taking a single, first step. For most people, talking to the COO of a fortune 100 company might be a little too much to start out with. That's ok. Start where you are. Make a list of 3-5 leaders that are closer to your proximity. Start with your boss or immediate supervisor, and see if you can get 2 or 3 more at the same level or at the next one up. Throughout my entire career, I always had a meeting every week or two with someone higher up. You would be amazed not only how much you can learn from someone in such a position, but also how quickly you can learn about their position.
2. Using Rule #2, No Blank Meetings, as described in Chapter 5, reach out and put time on one or two of those people's calendars. Then, show up. Setting a meeting is great, but only if you don't flake out. Nothing is worse than developing a reputation for scheduling meetings and then constantly bailing. Leaders time is precious, so is yours, treat both as such and you'll find it easy to talk to them when you need to.
3. Go through and do the 5 Steps to Create Opportunity as outlined earlier in this chapter. As I moved up in the organization, I found no shortage of people who wanted to talk to me. The ones who got to keep doing it, were the same ones that didn't waste my time. Anyone can get one meeting with a leader, it's getting them consistently that matters.
4. Cancel when needed. Although you don't want to make a habit of this, its not uncommon to run out of things to talk about. After all, most peoples jobs don't change that regularly. Or if it's about to be a long holiday weekend and you have nothing to talk about because you are pumped for what you and your friends have planned, don't make the mistake of making the leader stay late for a meeting. Contrary to popular belief, leaders have friends and holiday plans too. Treat their time with respect and they will be more inclined to do the same with yours.

5. Above all, try and enjoy talking to them. It sounds silly I know, but throughout my entire career I always had a mentor. Sometimes they were formal, other times it was more informal and we'd just go on a walk together once a week while we talked shop, asked questions and shared experiences. With so many people working remotely now, there has never been a better time to have remote happy hours or coffee chats. Learning on your own is great, but so is learning from others. Plus, learning from others often allows you to benefit from how they already organized the information. So reach out, schedule time and start benefiting from the collective knowledge of all the leaders already around you.

Conclusion

"It's a helluva start, being able to recognize what makes you happy."
- Lucille Ball

As the great Martin Luther King Jr. once said, "The ultimate tragedy is not the oppression and cruelty by the bad people but the silence over that by the good people." If the silence over bad people's behavior is the ultimate social rights tragedy of recent times, then the silent, albeit internal suffering of capable, educated, and hardworking people just like you is not only the greatest economic tragedy of our time, but the single biggest collective waste of our mental resources.

Although spending your days answering pointless emails, attending back-to-back meetings where nothing gets accomplished, and moving your mouse or sitting at your desk longer than needed to give the appearance you are working longer than you actually are might be effective ways to keep a job. They are certainly not the most effective ways to use your very limited amount of time. So often, I think we delude ourselves into thinking that the amount of time we spend at work is beyond our control. Using the few things in our lives that we genuinely like, we try using them to justify all of our day-to-day choices.

I believe the primary reason we do this is because of fear. Rather than admitting to ourselves we are scared to chase our dreams, we use bills, other people, our children (if you have them), and a whole host of other socially acceptable reasons why we continue to work for companies and in jobs that make us feel dead inside. We point to corporate managers, administrators, and other professionals who set the schedules as the reason we can't architect a life we love. We mutter to ourselves that *we should just be grateful for all that we have—we know how lucky we are when compared to countless others.*

For me, I'll never forget when these feelings became truly unbearable. Truth be told, they had been building for months, even years—but I, like you, had spent an entire lifetime practicing my ability ignoring them. On that fateful day, I was sitting in my sons' room, watching them both sleep soundly. Over the past week, this had become somewhat of a habit of mine. I noticed that watching them helped me ignore how I felt. It helped remind me why I woke up every day and went to a job that, by all accounts, was great but not for me. As I watched my two boys breathe in and out, their peaceful faces completely unaware of the inner turmoil in their father, I started imagining their future. Although it was filled with all the material things my great corporate career could provide, it was their emotional state that kept me up that night.

I started thinking quietly to myself, on their playroom floor, that If I felt this way, then what were the chances they would too? Furthermore, what role would I play in teaching them that appearing to have the American Dream, the house, the cars, and every material thing anyone could ever want was actually having *it*? How much responsibility would I have in teaching them, my two joyful and carefree little toddlers, that eventually becoming a burned-out, overworked, and underpaid adult was totally normal and just how things worked?

There is an old saying that says, "We do not inherit the earth from our ancestors; we borrow it from our children." If you have picked up this book and have made it this far, it's safe to assume you know something is wrong. You have a feeling deep down in your gut that there is more to life than how you are currently living it. Maybe there is more to your career than just doing what you're supposed to for as long as you are expected. Maybe there is more to being a good mother or a good father than just providing financially for your children.

I'll admit I don't have everything figured out, but I can tell you with certainty that once you start practicing the habits outlined within, allowing yourself more time to slow down, think, and question all that is around you, you are going to start seeing opportunity everywhere. In fact, the amount of things in this world that could be improved is practically endless, and by spending our time trying to be good corporate employees instead of improving those things, is the biggest waste of our

Conclusion

collective talents, passions, and lives. So, above all, if this book has done anything, I hope it's inspired you to stop ignoring how you feel deep down. Stop trying to be the best worker you can be and start trying to be the best human being. We are not efficient, and we are certainly not describable only through numbers, so why do we allow our economy, companies, and lives to be encapsulated as such?

How we view work and how our economy is measured is more than 100 years old, and managing your time better in order to work less and live more is the first step toward fixing it. Once you and millions like you have more time, there is no telling what problems we'll be able to solve, what art we'll be able to create, and what future we'll be able to build. That feeling deep down in your gut is trying to tell you something; maybe it's time you stop trying to do as much as possible in order to ignore it and just listen.

Acknowledgements

I HAVE A CONFESSION. I did not realize how big of a commitment writing a book was, until I found myself unemployed and staring at my computer screen. A huge, complex and often very messy endeavor I would of done it either way, I just don't think I would have started out so optimistic.

There is not enough space nor time to thank all those that helped me along my journey. That said, I would like to specifically thank those that helped make this book possible.

First and foremost, thank you to my young colleagues at Epsilon, who gave me the initial encouragement. I would never have had the guts to quit my job and jump in head first, had you not emphasized how excited you all were to read it.

Next, I'd like to thank my good friend Doug. Our weekly Wednesday hikes in the Mountains of Colorado, where we discussed ideas, concepts and business strategies were invaluable to helping me clarify my thinking. Thanks buddy. I owe you one and am already looking forward to our next hike.

Huge thanks to both Samantha Griswold and Danny Decilis for reading my early drafts, and being very gentle yet incredibly insightful with their feedback.

Shout out to my editor, Andrea - for patiently correcting every comma, misspelled word and confusing sentence.

Thanks to Lauren, for your incredible cover design, and your patience as I asked for countless revisions.

Thank you to my publishers at BookCrafters. This first time author is incredibly grateful for you taking him under your wing and showing him how to properly share a book with the world.

Lastly, I'd like to thank the leaders, managers and mentors that I have had the pleasure of working, learning from and collaborating with. It is

Acknowledgements

said no one achieves anything alone, and my career is a living testimony of all that you have done for me. During all our time together, I learned so much about data, business, and life, for which I am eternally grateful.

To everyone else left unmentioned, thank you for all that you did. It's true what they say, its take a village and this author is incredibly grateful for his.

Appendix A: Learnings While Working
(Updated as of Jan 2023)

- Learned Python coding language and built: a portfolio app, text game, and website.
- Learned JSON (node.js).
- Read and learned about the tax benefits of an LLC.
- Started an LLC.
- Built a browser and learned how they work.
- Built a simple dice iOS app. One of those, you shake the phone, and it rolls two six-sided dice.
- Learned the fundamental mathematical concepts behind machine learning.
- Built a Flask blog app.
- Built a Django web portfolio app.
- Learned about Elon Musk and the journey of X.com, to PayPal, to SpaceX, and to Tesla.
- Started three companies.
- Hired a freelance engineer to design a CAD model for a new invention I had in my head.
- Worked with manufacturers to produce an initial inventory of 300.
- Learned the basics of social media marketing and got 5K followers in 1 year.
- Learned and hired an assistant.
- Learned and raised $2K on Kickstarter.
- Shot a commercial for my product and company, working with producers and other video professionals.
- Hired friends to serve as my actors.
- Laid someone off when one of those companies failed.

Appendix

- Learned to admit I had failed publicly, then learned not to be ashamed of my failure.
- Read and learned the basics of creating a Minimal Viable Product (MVP).
- Learned the basics of stock market investing.
- Researched and learned about how the wealthy manage their money.
- Started actively investing.
- Read, researched, and learned about cryptocurrencies.
- Read and learn about public ledgers.
- Researched blockchain, gaining a rudimentary understanding.
- Started writing four books, one of which you just read.

www.ingramcontent.com/pod-product-compliance
Ingram Content Group UK Ltd.
Pitfield, Milton Keynes, MK11 3LW, UK
UKHW020047311224
452994UK00004B/382